How to Prepare and Give a Speech

BY
MICHAEL KRAMME, Ph.D.

D1568713

COPYRIGHT © 1996 Mark Twain Media, Inc.

Printing No. CD-1850

Mark Twain Media, Inc., Publishers
Distributed By Carson-Dellosa Publishing Company, Inc.

Table of Contents

Introduction

The purpose of this book is to introduce students to spoken communication as well as theatrical forms of communication.

Teachers may choose to use the readings and exercises as class projects or as extra enrichment activities for individual students. Students may do some of the activities independently. An oral presentation is recommended for many of the chapters. Any exercise that will requre the student to perform before an audience is labeled *Presentation*. Projects in the discussion and debate chapters are labeled as *Group Presentations*.

A set of questions appears after each narrative. These questions provide a quick check of reading comprehension. One or more activities also follow each narrative.

Communication

Communication is the transfer of a meaning from one being to another. Communication includes written and spoken words, symbols, movements, gestures, facial expressions, the tone of the voice, and anything else that can transfer meaning.

Four things must be present in order for communication to occur. There must be (1) a sender, (2) a receiver, (3) a message, and (4) a medium. The medium is the means or way by which the communication travels. The plural of medium is media. Mass media refers to the means by which communication occurs with a large number of receivers who may or may not be present at the site of the communication.

Communication occurs in many different ways. Non-verbal communication refers to communicating without using words. We can express meaning by a nod of the head, a shrug, or a facial expression. Even our posture or the way we walk can give others a message. At times, non-verbal messages may contradict the meaning of the words we are using.

Verbal communication is the sharing of meaning by using words. Both speaking and writing are verbal forms of communication. Most human communication is verbal.

Oral, or spoken, verbal communication takes many forms. Interpersonal communication takes place between two or more persons. This is the most common. Every time we talk to another person, we are using interpersonal communication. A similar word, intrapersonal, means communicating with ourselves.

Group communication is another common way of transferring information. This occurs when three or more people communicate together. Another word for group communication is discussion. This important means of communicating includes informal groups as well as more formal situations such as conferences, committee meetings, and workshops. Debate is an advanced, highly-controlled type of group communication.

Public communication is another major form of communication. This is when one person shares meaning with a group of people. A teacher giving a presentation in the classroom is using public communication. Anyone giving a speech to a group is also using public communication.

Specialized types of public communication include oral interpretation and theater. Oral interpretation is the reading of literature out loud to an audience. Theater involves a performer imitating, or pretending to be, someone else.

All of us communicate constantly. Even as you are reading this narrative, communication is occurring. We often take communication for granted, but communication skills are vitally important to survival. We communicate so often that we are seldom aware of the actual process, but we can study, practice, and improve our communication skills. We can all continue to learn to communicate more effectively.

Name _____ Date _____

Questions for Consideration

1. What is communication?

_____

2. What are the four things necessary for communication to occur?

_____

_____

_____

3. What is the plural of medium?

_____

4. What do we call means of communication to a large number of receivers who may or may not be present?

_____

5. What type of communication is a gesture or facial expression?

_____

6. What type of communication uses words, either spoken or written?

_____

7. What is communication between two people called?

_____

8. What is another word for group communication?

_____

9. What type of communication is used by a teacher speaking to a class?

_____

10. What is the major difference between a person giving a speech and an actor performing a role?

_____

11. What can we do to improve our communication skills?

_____

_____

Name _____ Date _____

Defining Communication Terms

1. Define *communication:*

_____

_____

Define the following types of communication:

2. Mass Media _____

_____

3. Non-verbal _____

_____

4. Verbal _____

_____

5. Oral_____

6. Interpersonal _____

_____

7. Intrapersonal _____

_____

8. Group Communication_____

9. Debate_____

_____

10. Public _____

11. Oral Interpretation_____

12. Theater _____

_____

4

Name _____ Date _____

Communication Crossword Puzzle

Use the clues below to complete the crossword puzzle. Answers can be found on the communication narrative page. .

ACROSS

1. The reading aloud of literature (two words)
6. One of the four parts of any communication; this is the way or means for communication
9. Using written or spoken words to communicate
10. Communication between three or more people
12. A highly-controlled type of group communication
13. One of the four parts of any communication; this is what is transmitted
14. One of the four parts of any communication; this transmits the communication

DOWN

2. Not using words to communicate (hyphenated word)
3. The performer imitating someone else
4. Another word for spoken
5. Communication with oneself
7. Communication between two people
8. One of the four parts of any communication; this gets the communication
11. Communicating to a large group who may or may not be present (two words)
15. Another word for group communication

Stage Fright

Stage fright, as the words imply, is the fear of appearing on a stage. It also refers to the fear of making a presentation in front of a group of people. Stage fright appears in a variety of situations. It can happen regardless of whether the person has memorized the material, rehearsed the presentation, or presented it without practice and preparation. It is not likely that a person will "get over" stage fright. However, with better understanding, stage fright is controllable.

The first step in lessening stage fright is to realize how common it is. Almost everyone has some degree of stage fright. It bothers some people much less than others, but it is still there. Extreme stage fright can cause physical reactions to occur. The stomach can become upset. We refer to this as "having butterflies in the stomach." Extra perspiration can occur. Some presenters tremble. Also, the mouth can become either very dry or very wet.

REMEMBER: ALMOST EVERYONE HAS STAGE FRIGHT. IF YOU HAVE IT, KEEP IN MIND THAT IT IS QUITE COMMON. YOU ARE NOT UNUSUAL OR DIFFERENT FOR HAVING IT.

As strange as it may seem, stage fright is actually beneficial. It is the body's way of giving us extra alertness and energy to face the task ahead. When humans face danger or a challenge, the body produces extra adrenaline. Adrenaline is a natural chemical that increases the energy needed to meet the challenge. Adrenaline stimulates circulation and relaxes muscles. It often takes a person time to relax after a time of danger, a public performance, or a sporting event. This is because the adrenaline produced to meet the challenge is still in the body's system.

REMEMBER: STAGE FRIGHT IS NATURE'S WAY OF HELPING FACE A CHALLENGE.

Presenters can do some things to help lessen the degree of stage fright they have. One thing that can help is to gain experience performing in front of a group. Often, with more experience, the stage fright lessens. Good preparation is another way of helping lessen the effects of stage fright. The more a speaker rehearses the presentation, the more confident and comfortable he or she will become. The better rehearsed the presentation is, the less chance that something can go wrong. Since there is less chance of a problem, there is less about which the speaker has to worry.

Another thing that helps lessen stage fright is to realize that it is natural, and not to worry about being nervous. It also helps for the speaker to know that in most situations the audience wants the speaker to be successful. The audience is not the enemy of the speaker: they are partners in communication.

When possible, physically relax before the presentation. Take a few deep breaths before going on. If you are out of the view of the audience, yawn a few times. Stretching and shaking the hands and arms loosely can also help with relaxation. The more you are able to relax, the less stage fright you will experience.

REMEMBER: THINGS CAN BE DONE TO LESSEN STAGE FRIGHT.

The effects of stage fright are always more noticeable to the speaker than the audience. Many times, the audience does not even notice the speaker's nervousness.

Name _____ Date _____

Questions for Consideration

1. What is stage fright?

_____

2. What is the first step to lessen stage fright?

_____

3. What is the phrase used to describe an upset stomach caused by stage fright?

_____

4. List three things that physically can happen to a speaker because of stage fright.

_____

_____

_____

5. What was the first important "remember" statement in the text?

_____

_____

6. What is the name of the chemical the body produces to help in time of challenge?

_____

7. What was the second important "remember" statement?

_____

_____

8. Name four things the narrative mentioned that a speaker could do to lessen stage fright.

_____

_____

_____

9. What was the third important "remember" statement?

_____

10. Who often notices the speaker's nervousness the most?

_____

Name _____ Date _____

An Art Activity

Project 1. Prepare a series of posters to illustrate the following major points from the narrative about stage fright:

- Almost everyone has stage fright. If you have it, keep in mind that it is quite common. You are not unusual or different for having it.
- Stage fright is nature's way of helping face a challenge.
- You can do things to help prevent stage fright.

Project 2. Prepare a series of posters illustrating the following ways of lessening stage fright:

- Realize how common stage fright is.
- Prepare well to help lessen stage fright.
- Practice the presentation.
- Remember, the audience is not the enemy.
- Relax physically.

Perhaps you could make a bulletin board display for the classroom with the posters.

An Essay: "My Brush with Stage Fright"

Everyone has experienced stage fright. One way to help overcome it is to better understand it. This essay may help you in your struggle to lessen stage fright. While writing the essay, attempt to "stand back" from the event, and try to look at the experience differently. Even though the experience was not funny at the time, try to view it with a sense of humor.

Using your own paper, write a one-page essay in which you describe a situation in which you had stage fright. Tell what the situation was, how stage fright affected you, and what you did about the stage fright.

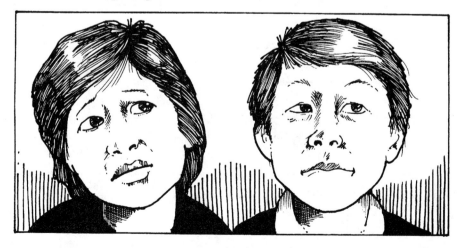

Interviewing

Interviewing is an important way to get information. Most interviews are a form of one-on-one communication. This means that one person, the *interviewer,* asks questions of another person, the *interviewee.* At times, a group may be the interviewers or interviewees, but this is less common. The interview provides information when other sources of material are not available. Many interviews are major events in people's lives. Some of the most important interviews that most individuals go through are interviews for jobs.

Many students interview an expert in the subject chosen for a speech or report. The interview should never be the first step in gathering information. It should take place only after other research has been completed. Early research will help the interviewer discover what information is lacking. This research will save time and allow the interview to focus on material that may not already be available.

The interviewer must prepare carefully to make the interview experience successful. A well-prepared list of questions will help keep the interview on the right track. Prepared questions also help get the interview started and keep it moving along smoothly. The questions prompt the interviewee's memory as well so that the interviewer can get all the important information needed.

A good interview depends on good questions. Careful wording of questions is critical to get at the important points of the subject. The questions should encourage the interviewee to discuss the material rather than just answer "yes" or "no." It is a good plan to have more questions prepared than would seem necessary. Having too many questions is better than having too few.

The interviewer must always be prompt. It is better to arrive five minutes early than one minute late. A good interviewer is always courteous. It is good to remember that the interviewee is doing a favor by giving up his or her time for the interview.

It is vital for the interviewer to take notes neatly and carefully. The notes must be clear and understandable when reviewed later. It is better to review the notes soon after the interview, because it is easier to remember details while they are still fresh in the memory.

When quoting from the interview, use the exact words of the interviewee. No one appreciates being misquoted. Many interviewers use a tape recorder. This allows for a more exact record of the conversation at the interview. The interviewer should always ask permission to record the conversation before doing so, since some interviewees are not comfortable talking when a tape recorder is used.

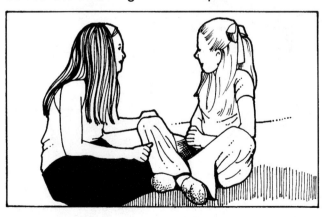

The interview should take enough time for thoroughness, but it should not be too long. The interviewer should never waste time. Courtesy is also important at the end of the interview. The interviewer should always thank the interviewee for his or her time and efforts. In most instances, a written thank you note is also appropriate.

9

Name _____ Date _____

Questions for Consideration

1. What is the definition of an interviewer?

_____

2. What is the definition of an interviewee?

_____

3. What is the type of communication for most interviews?

_____

4. What is one of the most important interviews that most individuals go through?

_____

5. What should always happen before the interview questions are written?

_____

6. What three things will questions written before the interview achieve?

_____

_____

_____

7. What should interview questions encourage the interviewee to do?

_____

8. What questions should be avoided for interviews?

_____

9. How many questions should be prepared for an interview?

_____

10. What is important about notes from the interview?

_____

11. When should the notes be reviewed?

_____

12. What is important to remember about using a tape recorder during an interview?

_____

_____

Name _____ Date _____

Preparing for an Interview

What is the topic of the interview? _____

Who is going to be the interviewee? _____

Why was this person chosen? _____

_____

Write three good questions that would be good background or starting questions.

1. _____

_____

2. _____

_____

3. _____

_____

What are four major pieces of information that are missing after the first research about the topic?

1. _____

2. _____

3. _____

4. _____

Write four questions about curious or unusual aspects of the subject. (Note: these should be open-ended questions, rather than yes/no or questions that need only short answers.)

1. _____

2. _____

3. _____

4. _____

Name _____ Date _____

Presentation: Making an Introduction

Step 1: Confer with your teacher to choose someone to introduce to the class. This could be a fellow classmate, a member of your family, a friend, or a complete stranger. The person whom you will introduce will not have to be present when you give the introduction.

Step 2: Prepare a set of interview questions.

Step 3: Have an interview with the person chosen as the subject of the introduction.

Step 4: Prepare the introduction. Remember to make it as interesting as you can. Be sure to stay within the time limits of the assignment.

Step 5: Practice your presentation so you are more comfortable with it.

Step 6: Present your introduction in front of the class.

Presentation: "In the Good Old Days"

Step 1: Confer with your teacher to choose a senior citizen to interview for an oral presentation to the class.

Step 2: Prepare a set of interview questions. Be sure to ask about differences between when the interviewee was a child and now. What are the differences in things such as clothing, school, customs, work, and daily life?

Step 3: Have an interview with the senior citizen. Be sure to thank him for his help.

Step 4: Prepare a presentation based on the interview. Remember to make it as interesting as you can. Be sure to stay within the time limits of the assignment.

Step 5: Practice your presentation so that you are more comfortable with it.

Step 6: Present your introduction in front of the class.

Name _____ Date _____

Presentation: Introducing Yourself

Some people find that it is more difficult to introduce themselves than it is to introduce someone else. Perhaps they are not comfortable talking about themselves. Others do not believe that they are interesting enough to be the topic of a speech. For this activity, you should prepare a short speech in which you introduce yourself to an audience. It is best to begin with a self-inventory.

What are three interesting things that you have done or that have happened to you?

1. _____

2. _____

3. _____

What are your hobbies or special interests?

1. _____

2. _____

3. _____

4. _____

What other places have you lived or visited?

1. _____

2. _____

3. _____

What other interesting things can you think of that you would like to share with others?

1. _____

2. _____

After completing this inventory, select the two or three things from the list that you believe would be the best to tell about in your speech. Do not try to include too many different topics within the speech. Now write out notes for your speech. It is better to use notes as reminders for your speech, rather than to write the entire speech out. Be sure to have a good introduction and conclusion prepared. Remember to practice before giving your speech!

Preparing to Give a Speech

Giving a speech to an audience is one of the more formal types of communication. Preparing a good speech requires extra effort. It is important to carefully craft the speech. In addition, the speaker must use proper presentation skills. The selection of a topic, research, and organization of materials is similar to that of writing an essay. The presentation skills, however, are completely different.

The speaker must choose a speech topic to fit the audience and the occasion. The speech should have a strong introduction. This gets the audience's attention. The body of the speech must be concise and well organized. This helps the audience follow and understand the speech.

Projection is speaking loudly and clearly. Clear speaking is a necessity. A speech cannot be successful if the audience cannot hear the speaker or cannot understand the words. Volume is of major importance. The speaker must project his or her voice so that everyone in the audience can easily hear.

Diction is another important factor. Diction is speaking clearly. The speaker should make sure to use every sound of the word distinctly. The best way to improve diction is to slow down. Many beginning speakers talk too fast. This is often because of nervousness. Another helpful skill in improving diction is to be sure to use all consonant sounds. This is especially true with final consonant sounds. The speaker needs to be sure to use the final "d", "t", and "ing" sounds of words.

Expression is speaking with an interesting voice. The speaker should use as much *vocal range* as possible. Vocal range includes using a variety of pitches (high and low sounds). *Inflection* is another part of expression. It is the pattern of curving or bending the sound of the words in a phrase. In English, we often use a rising inflection at the end of a question. Variety of expression will make the speech more interesting. Without variety, the speaker's voice will become monotonous.

The speaker must have good *eye contact.* This means looking at the audience. The speaker should use notes rather than writing the speech out. The audience should be "spoken to" not "read to." Eye contact helps the speaker connect with the audience. The audience then feels more a part of the communication.

Good *posture* helps the speaker give a positive impression to the audience. It helps communicate to the audience that the speaker is confident and has something of interest to say. A speaker should stand up straight but not be rigid. The speaker should keep his or her weight balanced evenly on both feet. The speaker should avoid shifting his or her weight from foot to foot. Having the weight on the ball of the feet, rather than the heels, helps the speaker to appear more involved in the speech.

Speakers should *not* use fillers. A filler is a sound or word that creeps into the speech. The most common filler is "ah." This often fills in a pause between thoughts. "And" or "and ah," and "I mean" or "you know" are other common fillers. The use of fillers can be a difficult habit to break. The speaker needs to listen for fillers while speaking. When the speaker hears them, he or she then must concentrate to leave them out of the presentation. Listening to a recording of the speech is another effective method of becoming aware of using fillers.

14

Name _____ Date _____

Questions for Consideration

1. What must a speaker be concerned with in addition to crafting the speech?

_____

2. What two things must the topic of a speech fit?

_____

3. What should the introduction of the speech achieve?

_____

4. What two things must the body of a speech be?

_____

5. What is projection?

_____

6. What is diction?

_____

7. What final sounds should the speaker take extra care to project?

_____

8. What does vocal range include?

_____

9. What does a rising inflection often indicate in spoken English?

_____

10. What happens to a speaker's voice without variety?

_____

11. How should the speaker stand?

_____

12. Why should a speaker keep the weight on the balls of his or her feet?

_____

13. What are "fillers" in a speech?

_____

Name _____ Date _____

Preparing to Give a Speech: Word Search

Find and circle the following words that are important in preparing a speech. The words may be written vertically, horizontally, or diagonally, and may be spelled forward or backward.

```
H O C C A S I O N D S O Q T X P E U A Q
I V C A E U Y H B M I J Z V C M W D E I
E C N E I D U A B Z F K X F U D S X H A
G C O N S O N A N T P X X L D P P V C P
L L O H F N R Z S A V S O E K R Q R L Q
M N H M H B E U E D C V Y V E I E Z D D
O N H Q M X U U L S A E O S F K R J H G
N I W E R U T S O P C Y S B A T Y C Y P
O D N Z Y C N Q B O D I F E M Y E F S I
T I A F Z T S I N V O N P S R E L L I F
O C O Y L V E T C N O S L E P Q V J E J
N T N T D E A I L A X C X S T W R M D L
O I K O L C C C R T T C A K T H B Y V N
U O F P T U D T E A U I D L S L O H K N
S N Y I A D E K I S V H O I R T P V C K
T X M C D A M V G O J B S N R A T C Q W
Y M O L N X B Y E Y N T S P U G N V B C
Z Q N O I T C E J O R P T Q M K W G G X
O Z C O V A O R G A N I Z A T I O N E Q
V T V F C T P P R E S E N T A T I O N T
```

WORD LIST

audience · communication · consonant · diction · expression · eye contact · fillers · inflection · monotonous · occasion · organization · posture · presentation · projection · speaker · speech · topic · variety · vocal range · volume

16

Choosing a Topic

Finding a good topic for a presentation is often the most difficult task for many speakers. The choice of the topic is of major importance. The right choice of topic will make the rest of the speech preparation and presentation much easier. A poor topic choice can create extra work and difficulty.

The first rule for making a good choice is to find something that already interests you. It will be extra hard to get others interested if the topic does not interest you. When the topic interests you, your enthusiasm for the subject can spread to your listeners.

While the topic is already chosen for most speeches, the speaker must select a topic in some situations. When this happens, how does a speaker choose the topic?

One approach to finding a topic is to do a self-interest inventory. This inventory of interests often gives the speaker an idea for a good topic. The speaker asks him or herself several questions that may lead to good suggestions. Typical questions often include the following:

What are my hobbies or special talents?
What are some interesting things that I have done?
What interesting places have I visited?
What books or newspaper and magazine articles have I enjoyed reading recently?
What careers interest me?
What famous people interest me?
About what have I always been curious?

After you complete the inventory, make a list of topics that appear in the inventory answers. Next, it is time to evaluate each possible topic. For each topic, ask the following questions:

How interested am I in this topic?
How interesting can I make the topic?
Can I make this interesting to my audience?
Can I locate enough information about the topic?
Is this topic appropriate to the speaking situation?

After considering the answers to these questions, it may be helpful to assign each topic a number rating from 1 (low) to 5 (high). Next, go back and review the topics rated four or five. One of these higher-rated topics may be the subject for which you are looking. Make your choice from the list of highest rated topics. Keep your notes from the inventory and rating for future use.

The next step in choosing a topic is to focus or narrow the topic. Many beginning speakers try to cover too much information in one speech. It is much better to take a smaller part of the topic and do a complete and thorough job. Find out what the time limit for the speech is going to be. Then narrow the topic so you can adequately cover it within the time limit.

Name _____ Date _____

Questions for Consideration

1. What does a *good* choice of topic do for the speaker?

_____

2. What does a *poor* choice of topic do for the speaker?

_____

3. What is the first rule of choosing a speech topic?

_____

4. What often happens when the speech topic interests you?

_____

5. What can a self-inventory do for a speaker?

_____

6. What are four frequently asked questions in the self-inventory?

_____

_____

_____

_____

7. What is the next step in choosing a topic after completing the inventory?

_____

_____

_____

8. What are three questions often asked in evaluating a topic?

_____

_____

_____

9. What is the next thing done to a topic once it is chosen?

_____

Name _____ Date _____

Choosing a Topic: Self-Inventory

Fill in the following blanks to help select a good speech topic.

What are your hobbies?

_____

What are your special talents?

_____

What other special interests do you have?

_____

What interesting places have you been?

_____

What were the topics of five books or newspaper and magazine articles that you have read?

_____

What careers interest you?

_____

What famous people interest you?

_____

Why do they interest you?

_____

What have you always wanted to know more about?

_____

From the responses above, write down about twelve words or phrases that are possible speech topics:

_____

_____

_____

Rate each of the above topics from 1 (low) to 5 (high) based on how interesting and appropriate you believe them to be for the speech. Place your rating number in front of each topic. From these, select which topic you believe will be the best one for your speech.

MY SPEECH TOPIC IS _____

Name _____ Date _____

Narrowing the Topic

What is your speech topic?

_____

What is the time limit for your speech?

_____

The next step is to narrow or focus your topic to fit the time limits of the speech. Do not try to cover too much information in the speech.

List three important things about the history of the topic:

_____

_____

List three or four of the most important things a listener should know about the topic:

_____

_____

_____

List three or four of the most interesting or unusual things about the topic:

_____

_____

_____

What other parts or subdivisions of the topic can you list?

_____

_____

Look over your responses above.

Can any one of these be used as the topic for your final speech? _____

Can you cover just one of these well within the time limit? _____

Can you further divide the topic? _____

THE FINAL TOPIC I HAVE FOCUSED ON IS _____

Methods of Organization

Once a speaker has identified the major points of the speech, it is necessary to choose the best method of organizing the information. Good organization will help the audience follow what the speaker has to say and will aid the audience in understanding the topic as a whole. Poor organization will often cause confusion.

Many different types of organization are available for the speaker to use. At times the method of organization is obvious. In other situations, more than one method may work well. The speaker must then choose one of the possible methods. If the speaker has difficulty using one method, it may be helpful to try a different way to organize the speech.

The rest of this page discusses the most common methods of organization. Remember that the best method for one topic may not work at all for another.

Chronological means in order of time. Chronological topics are discussed in terms of the order in which the events or steps take place. Speakers often use the chronological method when describing a process or presenting the history of a topic.

Spatial organization uses space or geographical areas as a guide. A speech about a school might discuss the classrooms, then the gymnasium, then the offices, then the cafeteria, and so forth.

Using the order of *importance* is another common means of organizing material. It may be best to discuss some topics by going from the least to the most important aspect of the topic. Discussion from most to least important is better for other topics.

As the name implies, the *cause and effect* method discusses the causes of a situation and then discusses what happens because of these causes. Speakers often use the cause and effect method of organization for scientific and political topics.

The *problem to solution* method is similar to the cause and effect method of organization. In this method, a problem is first identified, defined, and discussed. The next part of the speech discusses a possible solution or solutions.

In the *difficulty* method, the speaker uses the order of difficulty of the points to organize the material. It is similar in this way to the order of importance method. The speech may go either from least to most difficult, or from most to least difficult.

When using the *topical* approach, the speaker chooses one topic or aspect of the subject, then moves on to another. A speech about a city might include topics such as population, economics, government, geography, and so on.

Name _____ Date _____

Questions for Consideration

1. What will good organization of a speech often help the audience do?

_____

2. What will poor organization of a speech often cause?

_____

3. What is another word for "in order of time"?

_____

4. What is a typical topic that would use order of time?

_____

5. What word describes using geographical areas as a method of organization?

_____

6. What two types of organization are possible using the order of importance?

_____

7. What type of organization is often used in speeches about scientific and political topics?

_____

8. What type of organization is similar to cause and effect?

_____

9. What type of organization is similar to order of importance?

_____

10. What two types of organization are possible in this (see question 9) method?

_____

11. What type of organizational method uses topics or aspects of the subject as the means of organization?

_____

Name _____ Date _____

Methods of Organization

List two topics for which it would be appropriate to use each of the major methods of organization.

Chronological

1. _____

2. _____

Spatial

1. _____

2. _____

Importance

1. _____

2. _____

Cause and Effect

1. _____

2. _____

Problem to Solution

1. _____

2. _____

Difficulty

1. _____

2. _____

Topical

1. _____

2. _____

Name _____ Date _____

Organizing Your Speech

To complete this exercise you should have already chosen your topic and done your research. The next thing to do is to choose the method of organization that you believe is the most appropriate to use.

YOUR SPEECH TOPIC: _____

METHOD OF ORGANIZATION TO BE USED: _____

Write the major points of the speech topic on the back of this page or on another paper. Using the method of organization you have decided on, list three or four of the major points below in the order you would present them. After you have filled in these blanks, go back and write in the reason you have put each of the points in the order you chose.

FIRST MAJOR POINT: _____

_____

Reason for using this point in this order: _____

_____

SECOND MAJOR POINT: _____

_____

Reason for using this point in this order: _____

THIRD MAJOR POINT: _____

_____

Reason for using this point in this order: _____

FOURTH MAJOR POINT (if used): _____

_____

Reason for using this point in this order: _____

Name _____ Date _____

Methods of Organization: Word Search

Find and circle the following words that are important in preparing a speech. The words can be found written vertically, horizontally, or diagonally, and may be spelled forward or backward.

```
G  C  J  R  F  G  N  D  D  P  H  S  T  P  W  K  J  F  K  M
T  C  E  F  F  E  Z  Q  Z  B  S  I  F  H  B  C  A  U  S  E
G  D  F  C  L  A  D  I  C  P  M  Y  Q  I  L  M  T  F  D  F
N  E  M  I  I  T  K  I  H  E  J  S  O  S  J  Q  T  M  E  P
H  P  O  E  U  F  J  U  F  U  I  Z  T  T  Y  U  B  X  D  H
P  Z  S  G  P  C  I  N  H  F  I  M  P  O  R  T  A  N  C  E
Z  U  T  Z  R  A  O  T  O  T  I  H  Q  R  H  L  E  A  S  T
C  V  G  Z  O  A  G  N  N  I  S  C  T  Y  E  D  Y  M  N  T
H  R  N  B  B  F  P  I  F  E  T  H  U  V  Q  B  R  X  R  D
R  S  I  P  L  B  Z  H  I  U  I  U  F  L  E  S  Q  I  K  R
O  H  D  O  E  J  D  P  I  R  S  C  L  J  T  T  B  Z  C  M
N  E  N  L  M  B  Y  W  C  C  Y  I  S  O  K  Y  R  M  V  J
O  X  A  I  T  U  T  Y  H  K  A  F  O  R  S  S  A  K  R  V
L  L  T  T  H  M  T  B  O  I  R  L  W  N  M  I  Q  K  O  C
O  G  S  I  A  B  B  B  D  B  F  C  Y  M  B  R  J  S  T  N  I
G  Q  R  C  F  G  H  D  K  D  J  M  M  B  F  V  S  C  C  P
I  O  E  A  Y  K  B  U  T  W  L  X  V  W  T  A  W  A  E  O
C  L  D  L  L  A  I  T  A  P  S  Y  T  A  A  L  L  Q  P  T
A  X  N  V  Q  H  D  I  P  F  W  L  A  C  I  P  O  T  T  L
L  F  U  N  O  I  T  A  Z  I  N  A  G  R  O  P  P  X  Y  W
```

WORD LIST

cause	chronological	confusion	difficulty
effect	geographical	history	importance
least	most	organization	political
problem	scientific	solution	spatial
time	topic	topical	understanding

25

The Introduction of a Speech

A major challenge to any speaker is to create a good *introduction*. A good introduction will do three things:

- Get the audience's attention
- Introduce the subject
- Provide a smooth movement into the rest of the presentation

Many speakers believe that the introduction is the most important part of the speech. The first impression that the audience receives in the introduction will often influence their opinion of the rest of the speech.

The *attention device* is the first thing that the speaker says or does. The speaker must choose the attention device carefully. It sets the tone for the rest of the speech. It needs to grab the attention of the audience and make them want to listen to the rest of the presentation. The attention device may be an interesting or perhaps surprising piece of information. It could also be an interesting question or quotation. At times, an action is a good attention device. Be sure that the attention device is genuinely unusual or important. Avoid using something such as: "My speech is about . . ." or "Have you ever thought about . . . ?"

Speakers use a variety of ways to get the audience's attention. Humor is a popular method. Everyone enjoys humor. However, the speaker must be careful when using humor. The humor used must be funny. It is embarrassing to tell a humorous story and not have anyone laugh. Humor should also be appropriate to the speech topic and the speaking situation. Another often-used attention device is the story. An interesting story can grab the attention of the audience. The story, like humor, must be interesting as well as appropriate. A surprising or curious fact can also get the audience involved with the topic.

The *preview* is the next major part of a speech introduction. The preview prepares the audience to follow and better understand the rest of the speech. This gives the audience a hint as to what will follow. The preview is often a simple definition or explanation of the topic. In a longer speech, the preview often introduces the major points that the speaker will cover in the body of the speech. A good preview will make the audience **want** to hear the rest of the presentation.

The *transition* is typically the last part of any good introduction. A transition is a movement from one thing to the next. In a speech, this transition should move smoothly from the introduction materials to the main body of the presentation. Without the transition, the speech can seem rough and choppy. In a short speech, the transition is often only one sentence. A transition can be a paragraph in longer speeches. It is seldom longer than one paragraph. Good transitions are often difficult to achieve. Many speakers write the exact wording of the transition out to help them remember and keep the smooth flow of the speech.

26

Name _____ Date _____

Questions for Consideration

1. What three things should a good introduction do?

_____

_____

_____

2. What often influences the audience's opinion of the entire speech?

_____

3. What is the name given to the first thing a speaker says or does?

_____

4. What will a good beginning to a speech make the audience want to do?

_____

5. What are three common methods of getting the audience's attention?

_____

_____

6. What is the second major part of a speech introduction?

_____

7. What are two common ways of achieving the second major part of the speech introduction?

_____

_____

8. What is a transition in a speech?

_____

9. Usually, how long is a transition in a short speech?

_____

10. What will many speakers do to help them remember the transition in their presentation?

_____

11. What often happens to the speech if the transition is missing?

_____

Name _____ Date _____

Creating a Good Speech Introduction

What is the title or subject of this speech? _____

Attention Device

List five possible attention devices that would be good for this topic (give actual examples, do not just name the type of device):

1. _____

2. _____

3. _____

4. _____

5. _____

Circle the attention device that you believe would be the best one to use for this speech.

Preview

Write a three or four sentence preview of the body of the speech. Attempt to make the preview interesting enough that the audience will want to listen.

_____

_____

_____.

_____

_____

Transition

Write a one-sentence transition that will help the audience move smoothly from the introduction to the body of the speech.

_____

_____

The Body of a Speech

The *body* of the speech is perhaps the most important part of the presentation. It is where the speaker gives most of the information about the subject to the audience. The speaker must carefully organize and prepare the body of the speech for effective communication.

After researching the topic, the speaker must choose the main body points. Selecting the best number of major points is important. If the speech does not contain enough major points, it will lack depth. If the speech contains too many points, it will be difficult for the audience to remember them all.

A good rule to follow is that it is better to have a few, well-explained points than to have too many. The exact number of points to use varies greatly on the topic, length of time for the speech, the audience, and the situation. Three or four major points for a ten-minute speech is a good average.

The introduction of the speech should have (1) gotten the attention and focus of the audience, (2) introduced the subject matter, and (3) had a transition into the body of the speech. The body of the speech should then give the major points and clearly explain each of the points. The body should also include definitions of any words that may have a special meaning or that the audience may not understand.

The speaker must decide how to organize the materials for the speech after he or she has chosen the major points. A speaker can organize the speech in many different ways. Some common methods of organization include order of importance, chronological order (in order of time), spacial order, problem to solution, and cause and effect.

Each of the major body points should first be stated clearly and concisely. Many speakers use "guideposts" to help the audience better understand. Words such as "first" and "an important thing" often help guide the audience. Each of the main body points should be of about the same importance to the total speech.

Each major body point should have supporting materials to help the audience understand and remember that point. Supporting materials may include definitions, examples, and additional facts. The number and type of supporting materials will vary greatly depending on the speaking situation. Visual aids can often help guide the audience through the speech. Each major supporting point should be of about equal importance to the body point of which it is part.

When moving to the next major body point, words like "next," "another thing to know," or "also" help the audience realize that the speaker has moved on to another point. The speaker should use good supporting material for each of the main points throughout the speech.

Outlining the speech is often the best way to help get organized. This is especially true when preparing the body of the speech. The outline often helps the speaker realize the proper emphasis for the material. The outline can also show which of the major points may need additional supporting material.

Name _____ Date _____

Questions for Consideration

1. What often occurs if there are too few body points in a speech?

_____

2. What often occurs if there are too many body points in a speech?

_____

3. How many major body points are typically in a ten-minute speech?

_____

4. What are four common methods of organizing material in the body of a speech?

_____

_____

5. What are "guideposts" in a speech?

_____

6. What should each major point be in relation to the other major points?

_____

7. What do supporting materials do for a major point?

_____

8. What are three types of supporting materials?

_____

_____

9. What is the best way to help the speaker get organized?

_____

10. What two things can this method of organization help the speaker realize?

_____

_____

Name _____ Date _____

The Body of a Speech: Exercise

Choose and research the topic for your speech. Next choose three or four major points in the speech. If you have too many major points, you need to limit or narrow your topic. Sometimes just one of the major points of the selected topic could become the entire topic for the speech.

After each of the Roman numerals, write one of the major points of your speech. For the letters after each major point, write in the three most important things about the major point that will help the audience better understand the topic.

SPEECH TOPIC: _____

I. (first major point) _____

_____

A. _____

_____

B. _____

_____

C. _____

_____

II. (second major point) _____

_____

A. _____

_____

B. _____

_____

C. _____

_____

Name _____ Date _____

The Body of a Speech: Exercise (continued)

III. (third major point) _____

_____

A. _____

_____

B. _____

_____

C. _____

_____

IV. (fourth major point, if there is one) _____

_____

A. _____

_____

B. _____

_____

C. _____

_____

The Conclusion of a Speech

Just as a good dessert finishes a meal, a good *conclusion* puts the finishing touch on a speech. The preparation of the conclusion should receive special attention and care. It is often what the audience remembers most clearly.

A strong conclusion should always include a transition from the body of the speech to a good final statement. In a longer speech, the conclusion often also includes a review of the major points.

The transition is a sentence that helps move the audience smoothly from the information contained in the speech to the final thought or wrap up. An example of a transition is "We have just discussed the three major parts of a speech." The transition does not need to be long or detailed. However, the speaker should not just jump directly from the body to the conclusion.

The review, if included, is often just a restatement of the major points of the speech. Some speakers believe it is a good idea to tell the audience the major points three times. First, state the main points of the topic in a preview during the introduction. Next, state the points and explain them in the body of the speech. Finally, state the main points a third time in a review during the conclusion. There is seldom a need for this repetition in a shorter speech, however.

The *final statement* the speaker makes is often the most important in the entire speech. It leaves the audience with a final impression. Final impressions often last the longest. Speakers refer to the *final statement* by many different names. Some people call the final statement a clincher, wrap-up, oomph statement, or other such names. A strong final statement helps the effectiveness of the speech. A weak final statement will lessen the impact of the entire speech.

The final statement should be a strong, clear signal that the speaker has finished. The speech should never seem to fade out or run out of steam. The audience needs this strong signal that the presentation is complete.

The speaker may choose from many good possible endings. Common examples include a strong or surprising statement or fact, an interesting question or thought, or a challenge to the audience. When appropriate, a joke or humorous story may end the presentation. The speaker must take care that the joke is appropriate to the situation and related to the topic.

Poor conclusions include weak statements such as "Now you know about . . . (the topic)." Another poor conclusion is asking, "Are there any questions?" Often the speaker wants to answer any questions that the audience has. However, this sentence or a similar one should not be the end of the actual presentation.

It is not always easy to create a good conclusion. However, it is important enough to spend extra time and energy to find exactly the right one.

Name _____ Date _____

Questions for Consideration

1. What two things should the conclusion to a speech include?

_____

_____

2. What do the conclusions in longer speeches often contain?

_____

3. What helps the audience move smoothly from the body to the conclusion of the speech?

_____

4. How many times do some speakers believe that the speaker should tell the audience the major points of the topic?

_____

5. Where in the speech should the major points be stated?

_____

_____

6. What are three words or phrases sometimes used to refer to the final statement of the speech?

_____

_____

7. What often occurs if a speech has a weak final statement?

_____

8. What are four common types of final statements?

_____

_____

_____

9. What are two examples given in the narrative of weak final statements?

_____

_____

Name _____ Date _____

Preparing the Conclusion for Your Speech

What is the topic of your speech? _____

Write out three possible transition sentences that will help you lead the audience from the body of the speech into your conclusion.

1. _____

_____

2. _____

_____

3. _____

_____

Write out four possible concluding statements for the speech. The challenge is to make them as exciting and interesting as possible.

1. _____

_____

2. _____

_____

3. _____

_____

4. _____

_____

Now select what you believe to be the best transition. Which one did you choose?

_____

Next, select the final statement you believe will best conclude your speech. Which one did you choose?

_____

Presenting Information

The most common type of speech is the *informative speech.* As the name suggests, the purpose of the speech is to share information with the audience. The shared information should be new to the audience. If the audience has some knowledge of the topic, the information in the speech should be in greater detail or depth. Classroom presentations, reports at business or club meetings, and tour presentations are just a few examples of presentations to inform.

Speeches to inform may be about people, objects, and ideas, as well as methods and processes. Most speeches to inform use the following basic pattern.

The *introduction* gets the audience's attention and interest. It previews the topic of the speech. It then provides a transition to the body of the speech.

The *body* of the speech gives the information. The speaker presents each major point using as much supporting information as possible. The information presented in the body must be clear. The speaker must also organize the material carefully. This helps the audience follow the information. The speaker should not try to give too much information at one time. It is better to present less information thoroughly. This makes it easier for the audience to remember.

The *conclusion* should contain a transition. This moves the speech from the information in the body to the concluding statement. In longer speeches, the conclusion includes a review of the major points made. The conclusion should contain a good final statement to end the speech in a strong, positive manner.

The speaker should work to keep the attention of the audience throughout the presentation. The speaker can do this by arranging the material so that it keeps building interest. Showing the audience how the topic affects them or is important to them can also aid in keeping their attention.

An excellent way to help the audience remember the information in a speech is to use reinforcement. *Reinforcement* is giving the information and then strengthening or increasing the understanding with fresh additions. The speaker may use a variety of aids to reinforce the information.

Using visual aids is often helpful. As the speaker presents the information, a *visual aid* (something seen by the audience) will reinforce the information. The audience will remember more because they have heard the material and then seen it. Seeing reinforces what they have just heard.

The speaker may use other methods of reinforcement. The speaker may restate the information in another way or in other words. The speaker may give an example to illustrate the information. Giving a comparison of the information with something else will also help reinforce.

In addition, the speaker will connect better with the audience and thus hold their attention longer by using notes rather than a full manuscript. The speaker should not write out the entire speech, but instead should transfer his or her notes onto small cards. Small cards are better than a full sheet of paper, because they will not distract the audience as much. Cards are also less likely to show movement if the speaker trembles from nervousness. The notes should serve as reminders to lead the speaker through the material.

Name _____ Date _____

Questions for Consideration

1. What is the most common type of speech?

_____

2. What is important about the information in a speech if the audience has some knowledge of the topic?

_____

3. What are the three parts of the basic pattern of a speech?

_____

_____

_____

4. What should the speaker avoid presenting in the body?

_____

5. What must the speaker work to keep throughout the entire speech?

_____

6. What two things can the speaker do to achieve the goal in question #5?

_____

_____

7. What is reinforcement in a speech?

_____

8. Name two things a speaker can do to reinforce information in a speech.

_____

_____

9. What is a visual aid?

_____

10. Why is it better to use small note cards than a full sheet of paper?

_____

Name _____ Date _____

Presentation: A Speech to Inform

Each student should now be ready to give an informative speech.

Rating Sheet for Speech to Inform

This form may be handed to audience members to fill out either during or after the presentation.

SPEAKER'S NAME: _____

TOPIC OF THE SPEECH: _____

Rate the speech on each of the following points using this scale:

   1 – poor   2 – average   3 – good   4 – very good   5 – excellent

Rating

_____ Did the speaker get my attention at the very beginning of the speech?

_____ Did the beginning of the speech give a good introduction to the topic?

_____ Were the major points clear?

_____ Were the major points well supported?

_____ Was the conclusion effective?

_____ Was the final statement strong?

_____ Did the speaker keep my attention and interest?

_____ Did the speaker speak in a loud enough voice?

_____ Did the speaker talk clearly?

_____ Did the speaker look at the audience?

_____ How was the speaker's posture?

_____ TOTAL POINTS

Other things I liked about this speech were:

_____

_____

_____

Using Supporting Materials

Supporting materials help members of the audience better understand the topic of a speech. The speaker may use them to explain, clarify, define, and illustrate the main points. Supporting materials also help give the audience better confidence in the speaker.

The source of the supporting material is also of importance. The better the source is, the more valid the supporting material becomes. When using a source, it is important to ask such questions as, "Who gave the information?", "How do they know?", "Do they have any bias or reason to distort the materials?"

Books, newspapers, and magazines are the most commonly used sources of material. Interviews, brochures, government documents, and other printed materials can also be helpful.

Speakers may use a variety of supporting materials. Common types of supporting materials include:

- **facts.** Facts are bits of information that can be verified or proven. Facts are the most commonly used type of supporting material.
- **statistics.** Statistics are bits of information presented as numbers.
- **descriptions.** Descriptions are explanations. They often show the relationships of the parts to the whole.
- **definitions.** Definitions give meaning to new, unclear, or specialized words.
- **quotations.** Quotations are examples of repeating what someone else has said. When quoting, the speaker should repeat the person's exact words.
- **comparisons and contrasts.** Comparison shows the similar parts of two different things. Contrasts show how they differ. This type of supporting material is often helpful when something familiar is compared or contrasted with something unusual or confusing. Special types of comparisons include similes, metaphors, and analogies.
- **restatement.** Restatement is saying something again, using other words. This type of repetition of the point can clarify meaning.

It is best if each major point of the speech has at least two or three pieces of supporting material. When possible, the speaker should try to include a variety of types of support. The use of variety will help keep the audience's interest.

Name _____ Date _____

Questions for Consideration

1. What two things will supporting materials help the audience members do?

_____

_____

2. What makes a piece of supporting material more valid?

_____

3. What is the most common type of supporting material?

_____

4. What are statistics?

_____

5. Between what do descriptions show relationships?

_____

6. What type of word used in a speech would need a definition?

_____

7. What should the speaker use when quoting someone?

_____

8. What do comparisons show between two or more things?

_____

9. What do contrasts show between two or more things?

_____

10. What are three special types of comparisons?

_____

11. What is a restatement?

_____

12. How many pieces of supporting material should a speaker use for each major point of a speech?

_____

Name _____ Date _____

Using Supporting Materials: Vocabulary

The following is a list of words used in the narrative about supporting materials. Look each of them up in a dictionary and copy the meaning on this sheet. After the meaning, write a sentence using the word appropriately, or give an example of the word.

1. Valid_____

_____

2. Bias _____

_____

3. Distort _____

_____

4. Brochures _____

_____

5. Verified _____

_____

6. Simile _____

_____

7. Metaphor _____

_____

8. Analogy _____

_____

9. Clarify_____

_____

10. Familiar _____

_____

Name _____ Date _____

Using Supporting Materials: Crossword Puzzle

Use the clues below to complete the crossword puzzle. Answers can be found on the narrative page dealing with supporting materials.

ACROSS

1. Resaying something using other words
4. Using several different types of support
8. The better the _____ , the more valid the supporting material becomes.
9. Bits of information that can be proven
11. Having belief in something
15. Information presented as numbers

DOWN

2. A special type of comparison
3. Repeating what someone else has said, using the same words
5. A source that relies on asking questions of an authority on a subject
6. Explanations that show relationships of the parts to the whole
7. Each major _____ should have at least two or three pieces of supporting material.
10. A reason to distort materials
12. Books, _____ , and magazines are the most commonly used sources of material.
13. Showing differences between two or more things
14. Showing the similar parts of two different things

Persuasion

Every day we are bombarded by persuasion. Others constantly try to get us to do something or to think a certain way. It is necessary for all of us to understand persuasion. This understanding can help us to persuade others. It can also help us to make better decisions and choices in our own lives.

The main purpose for a speech to inform is to give new information to others. The main purpose of a speech to *persuade* is to change the beliefs, attitudes, or behavior of the listeners.

One purpose of a speech to persuade is to *actuate.* This means to get the audience to **do something** rather than just think about the topic. Television commercials do this when they try to get the audience to go out and buy the product being advertised.

The basic structure of a speech to persuade is the same as that of a speech to inform. Both types of speeches need a good introduction with an attention-getting beginning. They both have a body where the speaker gives the main points of the subject. Each main point needs supporting material. Both types of speeches need to finish with a strong conclusion.

The persuasive speech, however, should always have a clear *thesis statement.* The thesis has two parts: the purpose and the topic. Examples of thesis statements are: "to persuade my audience (purpose) that smoking is bad for their health (topic)" and "to actuate my audience (purpose) to get a hobby (topic)."

The persuasive speech needs additional thought and preparation. It is a good idea to do an *audience analysis* before preparing a speech to persuade. This analysis tries to discover who the audience members will be. It also attempts to find out about their current beliefs. This information helps the speaker decide how to work with the subject material of the speech. When the speaker knows about the audience, he or she can decide how to best motivate the audience to listen and be persuaded.

A good persuasive speech will actively involve the audience. It will show how the topic affects them. When the audience knows the topic will affect them, they will listen more carefully. All of us have many needs. The speaker needs to relate the topic of the speech to at least one of these needs.

Basic human psychological needs include self-fulfillment. Self-fulfillment is doing something that will help the person develop into what they wish to become. Self-esteem is another basic psychological need. All of us need to feel good about ourselves. Reputation, achievement, status, and fame are all part of self-esteem. Everyone also needs to believe that they belong and are loved. Other basic human needs include safety and freedom from fear. Physical needs such as food, clothing, shelter, fresh air, and water are also major human needs. The speaker will have a better chance of persuading the audience when he or she can show that the thesis of the speech will meet one or more of these needs.

The speaker must take extra care when using supporting material. He or she must have good evidence and should use specific examples. The materials used must be strong and reasonable. The speaker must also demonstrate that he or she knows about the topic. The speaker should also convince the audience that he or she is honest and sincere when speaking about the topic.

Name _____ Date _____

Questions for Consideration

1. What two things can a better understanding of persuasion do for us?

_____

_____

2. What is the main purpose of a speech to persuade?

_____

3. What is the purpose of a speech to actuate?

_____

4. What are the two parts of a thesis statement?

_____

5. What two questions does an audience analysis try to answer?

_____

_____

6. Why is it important to show the audience how the topic will affect them?

_____

7. What is meant by self-fulfillment?

_____

8. What basic human need includes reputation, achievement, status, and fame?

_____

9. What are examples of basic physical human needs?

_____

10. What type of examples are needed in a speech to persuade?

_____

11. What three things must the speaker demonstrate about himself or herself to the audience in order to be an effective speaker?

_____

_____

Name _____ Date _____

Basic Human Needs

Define and give two examples that would meet each of the following basic human needs.

Self-fulfillment

Definition: _____

First example: _____

Second example: _____

Self-esteem

Definition: _____

First example: _____

Second example: _____

Belonging

Definition: _____

First example: _____

Second example: _____

Safety

Definition: _____

First example: _____

Second example: _____

Physical

Definition: _____

First example: _____

Second example: _____

Name _____ Date _____

Worksheet for a Speech to Persuade

Thesis Statement: To _____ my audience that they should _____ .

First major point: _____

_____

What basic human need does this point help fulfill?

_____

Supporting material:

    1. _____

    2. _____

    3. _____

Second major point: _____

_____

What basic human need does this point help fulfill?

_____

Supporting material:

    1. _____

    2. _____

    3. _____

Third major point: _____

_____

What basic human need does this point help fulfill?

_____

Supporting material:

    1. _____

    2. _____

    3. _____

Name _____ Date _____

Presentation: A Speech to Persuade

Each student should now be ready to give a persuasive speech.

Rating Sheet for a Speech to Persuade

This form may be handed to audience members to fill out either during or after the presentation.

Speaker's name: _____

Thesis of the speech: _____

Rate the speech on each of the following points, using this scale:

1– poor   2 – average   3 – good   4 – very good   5 – excellent

Rating

_____ Did the speaker get my attention at the very beginning of the speech?

_____ Did the beginning of the speech give a good introduction to the topic?

_____ Were the major points clear?

_____ Were the major points well supported?

_____ Did the speaker relate the topic to any basic human needs?

_____ Was the conclusion effective?

_____ Was the final statement strong?

_____ Did the speaker keep my attention and interest?

_____ Did the speaker speak in a loud enough voice?

_____ Did the speaker enunciate clearly?

_____ Did the speaker look at the audience?

_____ How was the speaker's posture?

_____ Was the speaker honest and sincere?

_____ Did the speaker seem to know the subject well?

_____ **TOTAL POINTS**

Using Visual Aids

Visual aids are things shown to the audience during a speech. They are helpful tools to assist the audience in understanding the speaker's message. Commonly-used visual aides include illustrations such as cartoons, charts, graphs, maps, pictures, and posters. Other visual aids are models, the objects themselves, and the speaker. Speakers often use equipment such as projectors and televisions to present visual aids.

Visual aids help reinforce the message. The audience receives the spoken message, and the visual aid gives them a visual message at the same time. We often understand more clearly and remember better what we see.

Remember, these are *aids.* They should not become more important than the speech itself. The visual aids should always fit the speech. The speaker should not use them just for the sake of having something to show.

The first thing to remember about using visual aids is that they must be visible to the audience. This means that they need to be large enough for the entire audience to see. The appropriate size of the visual aid will depend on the size of the audience and the room in which the speech will be given. It is important that the speaker does not block the view of any part of the audience. The speaker must always stand to the side of or behind the visual aid.

Visual aids should not be handled by the audience. They may accidentally break or damage an aid. Also, the audience will become distracted from the speech as they hand the aids from person to person.

The speaker should show the visual aids to the entire audience at exactly the time in the speech when each aid is illustrating a specific point. If the audience hands an aid around, each member will see it at a different time. It is often a good idea to keep the visual aids hidden or covered until the speaker needs them. This helps keep the audience's attention focused on the speech until the right moment. When the speaker shows an aid, the attention is then on the aid as the speaker makes the point.

Most visual aids used in a speech are made by the speaker. It is worth the extra time and effort to make the visual aids as clean, neat, and attractive as possible. Great artistic talent is not necessary to create good and effective aids.

A visual aid should not contain too much information. It may become too cluttered and confusing. It is better to make two or three charts, each showing one aspect of the topic.

Remember to practice using visual aids before the speech. The speaker needs to be familiar with each visual aid he or she is going to use. It is embarrassing if a visual aid does not work correctly during the speech. We have seen many "bloopers" on television where visual aids break or fall down. The chance of something similar happening is lessened when the speaker has practiced using the aid. Even with practice, things do go wrong, so the speaker should always have a back-up plan in case the visual aid does not work.

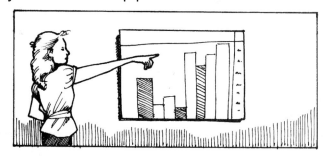

Name _____ Date _____

Questions for Consideration

1. What are visual aids?

_____

2. What do they help do?

_____

3. What type of message do the visual aids give?

_____

4. What should the visual aids always fit?

_____

5. What is the first important thing the narrative gives to remember when using visual aids?

_____

6. What will help determine the appropriate size of the visual aid?

_____

7. Where should the speaker stand while using a visual aid?

_____

8. What are two important reasons the audience should not handle a visual aid during the speech?

_____

_____

9. When should the speaker show the visual aid?

_____

10. What three things should the creator of a visual aid attempt to achieve when making the aid?

_____

_____

11. Why should a visual aid not include too much information?

_____

12. Why should the speaker practice with the visual aid?

_____

Name _____ Date _____

An Art Project

Create one or more effective charts, graphs, maps, or illustrations for a speech to inform or demonstrate. If you are giving a speech, make the aid for that presentation. If you are not giving a speech, choose a topic that would be appropriate as the subject of a speech.

Make sure that the visual aid will help assist the speaker in making a point clearer and more easily understood by the audience.

REMEMBER:
• You do not have to be an artist to make an effective visual aid.
• Keep the aid neat and clean.
• Do any lettering carefully.
• Make the aid as attractive as possible. Using bright colors adds to the look of the aid.
• Avoid putting too much information on one visual aid.
• Make sure the visual aid that you create is large enough to be seen by the entire audience.

An Alternative Art Project

In many instances, a model is an excellent visual aid. A model often takes more time and effort to create, but the extra efforts are often rewarding.

The model may be the actual size of the object, or the creator may enlarge the model so that the entire audience may see something that would otherwise be too small to observe. Likewise, if the object is one that is too large to use, such as a rocket or airplane, a smaller model would be effective.

Use the same reminders listed in the first project. When making a model, you should consider the following additional hints:

• Use durable materials to lessen the chance of damage.
• Often a cut-away version is helpful to show a cross section.
• At times, it is useful to use more than one model, each one showing a different stage of development or a different aspect of the topic.

Doing a Demonstration

A speech to *demonstrate* is a specialized type of speech to inform. The major difference is that though the speech to inform **tells** the material, the speech to demonstrate **shows and tells** it. Demonstration speeches are quite common. Many television shows include demonstrations. Cooking, craft, gardening, home repair, and building shows usually include demonstrations.

Most demonstrations present the steps in a process. The organizational method for them is often chronological. They tell the steps of a process in order of time. They show a sequence (first this happens, then this, this is next, and so forth).

Demonstrations are often effective because of reinforcement. The audience **hears** the words, and the words are reinforced by what they **see**.

Demonstration speeches are often the most fun of any type of speech. They can be fun to do and fun to watch. Many speakers also believe that demonstration speeches are easier. The speaker may be more at ease because the audience has its attention focused on the visual aids rather than on the speaker. The speaker needs fewer notes for a demonstration. The visual aids often remind the speaker of the next part of the speech.

All demonstrations use visual aids. Visual aids are whatever the audience sees during the demonstration. Commonly-used visual aids include charts, graphs, maps, pictures, models, and slides. Objects are also good visual aids. In demonstrating how to bake a cake or make cookies, the ingredients, bowls, pans, and so forth all become visual aids. The speaker may become a visual aid. This happens when the speaker shows how to do something like lead a cheer, do an exercise, or do the latest dance.

The speaker should remember that the visual aid is not more important than the speech. The speech should always be the major concern. The visual aid is there only to help and support the speech. It is to help the speaker communicate effectively.

The topic for a speech to demonstrate should not be too simple. It should not be something that most members of the audience already know how to do, either. Likewise, the topic for the demonstration should not be too complicated. It must be something that the speaker will be able to do clearly in the amount of time available.

Demonstrations often require more rehearsal than speeches to inform. The speaker must take care so that the audience can see any visual aid. The visual aid must be large enough for the entire audience to see. The speaker must not stand in front of the visual aid while speaking. The speaker must also be sure that all of the parts of the visual aid are there and are in working order.

The speaker also needs to practice with any visual aids to be used in the speech. This lessens the chance of something going wrong during the speech. It is embarrassing if the visual aid does not work properly. Other problems include visual aids that do not stay in

 place or keep falling down during the speech. The chances of problems with the visual aids lessens with practice. However, the speaker should always be prepared with another plan if the visual aid does not work.

Name _____ Date _____

Questions for Consideration

1. A demonstration is a specialized type of what kind of speech?

_____

2. What does the speech to demonstrate do in addition to telling information?

_____

3. What steps will a demonstration often show?

_____

4. What is the most common way to organize a speech to demonstrate?

_____

5. What two things cause reinforcement in a demonstration?

_____

6. Where is the audience's attention usually focused during a demonstration?

_____

7. Why does a speaker often use fewer notes in a speech to demonstrate?

_____

8. What are visual aids?

_____

9. What should the visual aids help the speaker do?

_____

10. What two things should the topic for a demonstration never be?

_____

_____

11. What must the speaker remember to avoid doing while using the visual aid?

_____

12. Why is it important to rehearse using a visual aid?

_____

13. What does the speaker need to have if something goes wrong?

_____

Name _____ Date _____

Worksheet for a Speech to Demonstrate

Topic: _____

First major point: _____

_____

Supporting material:

    1. _____

    2. _____

    3. _____

List any visual aids to be used to support this point. _____

Second major point: _____

_____

Supporting material:

    1. _____

    2. _____

    3. _____

List any visual aids to be used to support this point. _____

Third major point: _____

_____

Supporting material:

    1. _____

    2. _____

    3. _____

List any visual aids to be used to support this point. _____

Name _____ Date _____

Presentation: A Speech to Demonstrate

Each student should now be ready to give a demonstrative speech.

Rating Sheet for a Speech to Demonstrate

This form may be handed to audience members to fill out either during or after the presentation.

Speaker's name: _____

Topic of the speech: _____

Rate the speech on each of the following points, using this scale:

   1– poor   2 – average   3 – good   4 – very good   5 – excellent

Rating

_____ Did the speaker get my attention at the very beginning of the speech?

_____ Did the beginning of the speech give a good introduction to the topic?

_____ Were the major points clear?

_____ Were the major points well supported?

_____ Was the conclusion effective?

_____ Was the final statement strong?

_____ Was the topic an appropriate one, not too simple yet not too complex?

_____ Did the speaker use the visual aids effectively?

_____ Could I see the visual aids clearly?

_____ Did the speaker keep my attention and interest?

_____ Did the speaker speak in a loud enough voice?

_____ Did the speaker enunciate clearly?

_____ Did the speaker look at the audience?

_____ How was the speaker's posture?

_____ **TOTAL POINTS**

Special Occasion Speeches

Special occasion speeches include a variety of types. Their purpose is to honor persons or celebrate special achievements and events. They include information, but the main purpose is to honor, inspire, or challenge. Below are listed some of the more common special occasion speeches.

Introducing a speaker. One person often introduces the main speaker to the audience. This introduction is a common special occasion speech. The purpose of this speech is to gain the audience's attention and to get them interested in the speaker and his or her presentation. The introduction should give the topic of the speech. It also tells the background of the speaker. The introduction should also tell why the speaker is an authority on the topic.

The introduction should be short. The audience came to hear the speaker, not the introduction. It should mention the topic without going into too much detail. The person making the introduction should praise the speaker, but not too highly. Too much praise might embarrass the speaker and make the audience expect more than they should.

Presentation of an award. Many award shows appear on television each year. Clubs and organizations also present awards for a variety of achievements. Everyone who makes an award presentation is giving a special occasion speech. A presenter of an award should consider doing two things. First, the speaker could give a description of the award and its importance. Also, the speaker may include the reason for this presentation. This tells why the person is receiving the award. Presentation speeches are usually quite short.

Accepting an award. Some acceptance speeches are quite brief, perhaps just a "thank you." Other acceptances may be longer. The acceptance speech should thank those who selected the winner. The recipient of the award often says a "thank you" to others who have helped with the achievement. The speaker should not talk too long. The speaker must take care to avoid boring the audience with too long of a list of helpers. The acceptance speech also often conveys the feelings of the person getting the award. The receiver should not overestimate or underestimate the importance of the award, and he or she should work hard to avoid clichés.

Speech to honor. A speech to honor includes a variety of types, some of which are listed below.

Eulogy: a speech honoring someone who is no longer living.

Farewell: a speech honoring someone who is retiring or leaving an organization or group.

Dedication: a speech that dedicates an object or building to a person or cause.

Commemoration: A speech that remembers a special event.

Commencement: A speech that honors the graduates of a program. It often inspires or challenges the recipients as they continue their lives.

All of the types of speeches to honor have some common things to remember. The speaker should show the audience why the subject of the presentation should be important to them. The speaker should also give the reason for the tribute.

Name _____ Date _____

Questions for Consideration

1. What are the two major purposes of a special occasion speech?

_____

_____

2. What are the two major purposes of a speech to introduce a speaker?

_____

_____

3. What two things should a speech of introduction tell about the speaker?

_____

_____

4. What two things are often included in a speech to present an award?

_____

_____

5. Usually, how long are award presentations?

_____

6. What should the receiver of an award avoid doing when thanking those who helped?

_____

7. What is a eulogy?

_____

8. What is a commemoration?

_____

9. What two things does a commencement speech often do to the recipients of the degrees?

_____

10. What should a speaker giving a special occasion speech show the audience?

_____

_____

Name _____ Date _____

Vocabulary

Use a dictionary to define the following terms. Then write a sentence correctly using the word.

1. Acceptance _____

_____

2. Cliché _____

_____

3. Convey _____

_____

4. Eulogy _____

_____

5. Inspire _____

_____

6. Occasion _____

_____

7. Recipient _____

_____

Give an Example

Give a title for an example of each of the following types of special occasion speeches:

1. Eulogy _____

2. Farewell _____

3. Dedication _____

4. Commemoration _____

5. Commencement _____

Name _____ Date _____

Presentation: Presenting an Award

NOTE: Perhaps you could work with a partner on these presentations. You could present the award to your partner, and have him or her give an acceptance speech.

For this presentation you may pretend that you are presenting a real award (such as the Noble Prize for Literature, the Academy Award, the Emmy, or some such) or you may make up your own award.

Name of the award: _____

Name of recipient: _____

Describe the award: _____

_____

_____

Why does the recipient deserve this award? _____

_____

Presentation: Accepting an Award

Prepare a brief acceptance of an award.

Name of the award: _____

Whom will you thank? _____

Who gives the award and who makes the decision? _____

_____

Who has helped you be worthy of this award? _____

_____

What does this award mean to you? Why is it important? _____

_____

Name _____ Date _____

Presentation: Giving a Eulogy

Select the person whom you wish to eulogize. After doing research on the person's life, fill in the blanks on this page to use as your notes.

Person chosen to eulogize: _____

Introduction:

Attention step (the first thing you will say, it should get the audience's attention):

_____

Transition (the sentence that moves the speech smoothly into the body of the information):

_____

Body (list the major achievements or points of interest in the life of the person):

1. _____

_____

2. _____

_____

3. _____

_____

4. _____

_____

5. _____

_____

Conclusion (be sure to end with a strong finish):

_____

_____

_____

Name _____ Date _____

Presentation: A Dedication or Commemoration

You may choose to either dedicate an object or a building to a person, or you may commemorate a special event.

Subject of the presentation: _____

Introduction:
Attention step (the first thing you will say, it should get the audience's attention):

_____

Transition (the sentence that moves the speech smoothly into the body of the information):

_____

Body:
What are the reasons we should dedicate or commemorate this?

1. _____

2. _____

3. _____

What is the background or history for this event?

1. _____

2. _____

3. _____

4. _____

Conclusion (be sure to end with a strong finish):

_____

_____

_____

_____

Discussion

Group discussion is the most common type of interpersonal communication. Every time two or more people gather to talk, they are having a *discussion*. A discussion is a *dialogue* when only two people participate. When three or more people talk together, it becomes a *group discussion.*

A discussion may be for social enjoyment or simply to share information. Other discussions attempt to answer a question, solve a problem, or reach a decision.

Many group discussions are informal. Most of your conversations with friends are informal discussions. Other group discussions are quite formal and require careful planning. Formal discussion groups include business meetings, governmental meetings, and committee meetings.

Group discussions are important because they give the participants an opportunity to share their own views. Perhaps group discussions are more important because they also allow the participants to hear others' views. It is easier to find the best solution or to make the best decision based on a variety of information and viewpoints.

Successful discussions need good cooperation. All members of the committee must work together for a common purpose. The members of the group may disagree on many points, but they must work together.

A group often chooses a discussion leader. The primary task of the leader is to keep the discussion moving in an orderly way. This includes seeing that everyone in the group has an equal opportunity to participate. Another task of the discussion leader is to keep the group from straying away from the task or topic.

A *committee* is a special form of group discussion. The committee is a small group of people chosen from a larger group. It is easier for the smaller group to discuss, explore, and make decisions than it would be for the entire group. The committee has a specific chore or chores to do for the larger group. Many times the committee will make actual decisions on behalf of the entire group. Other times, the committee will recommend something back to the larger group. The large group often forms many committees, each one of them with a specific duty.

A *round table* discussion gets its name from the fact that the members gather around a table so that all people in the group can easily see each other. Round table groups share information and ideas for the benefit of the participants. This type of group seldom shares the results of the discussion with others.

A *panel* is a group discussion held for the benefit of an audience. In a panel discussion, the information discussed is for the benefit of the members of the audience as well as the panel members.

A *symposium* is similar to a panel discussion. Each member of the symposium presents a short prepared speech to the group. The symposium may include a discussion after the presentations are completed. However, many symposiums do not include any real discussion.

Name _____ Date _____

Questions for Consideration

1. What type of communication is group discussion?

_____

2. What is the name of a discussion between two people?

_____

3. What is the name of a discussion between three or more people?

_____

4. Name two reasons group discussions are important.

_____

_____

5. What is always necessary for a successful group discussion?

_____

6. What must all members of a group discussion work together to achieve?

_____

7. What is the primary task of a group discussion leader?

_____

8. What must the group leader be sure to do for each member of the group discussion?

_____

9. What is a committee?

_____

10. What is a round table discussion?

_____

11. What is a panel?

_____

12. What is a symposium?

_____

13. Which type of group discussion is only for the benefit of the members of the group itself?

_____

Name _____ Date _____

Discussion: Word Search

Find and circle the following words that are important in group discussions. The words are written up, down, or diagonally. They may be spelled forward or backward.

```
F  V  P  T  D  X  M  I  Y  U  Q  S  C  N  C  T  D  O  B  P
T  I  N  O  I  T  A  M  R  O  F  N  I  M  O  V  B  C  K  M
P  D  Z  E  T  I  N  F  O  R  M  A  L  T  N  O  N  J  C  V
Y  J  C  G  Y  Y  B  P  E  T  B  B  V  S  V  N  O  L  O  B
L  U  O  D  O  F  C  X  U  I  M  G  X  G  E  B  I  A  O  W
P  W  M  Q  M  G  O  Z  R  O  F  R  O  N  R  B  S  N  P  Q
T  Z  M  R  K  L  S  O  J  Q  R  Z  V  I  S  L  S  O  E  H
P  M  U  O  E  Q  P  A  N  E  L  G  J  T  A  P  U  S  R  H
L  E  N  Y  L  H  F  H  Q  H  T  Q  W  E  T  P  C  R  A  Y
R  N  I  O  B  E  E  O  R  H  H  P  U  E  I  U  S  E  T  S
L  Q  C  C  A  U  Q  R  R  E  W  L  V  M  O  T  I  P  I  Y
X  H  A  O  T  G  X  S  A  M  D  G  R  V  N  N  D  R  O  M
I  B  T  M  D  O  E  N  I  H  A  A  G  W  Z  Z  A  E  N  P
E  B  I  M  N  L  N  G  B  H  S  L  E  G  K  W  P  T  D  O
J  C  O  I  U  A  B  X  R  W  K  W  X  L  G  P  V  N  N  S
J  Y  N  T  O  I  L  I  A  S  T  N  I  O  P  W  E  I  V  I
Z  A  P  T  R  D  I  Y  E  J  Y  D  L  O  J  Q  V  Z  Y  U
F  C  Q  E  H  T  N  E  M  Y  O  J  N  E  P  R  C  M  H  M
V  L  M  E  V  W  I  R  J  X  O  S  F  M  Q  F  T  N  H  Q
V  E  Q  U  A  L  O  P  P  O  R  T  U  N  I  T  Y  E  V  Q
```

WORD LIST

committee   communication   conversation   cooperation
dialogue   discussion   enjoyment   equal opportunity
formal   group   informal   information
interpersonal   leader   meetings   panel
round table   share   symposium   viewpoints

Name _____ Date _____

Problem Solving

The primary task of a group discussion is to solve a problem. A common method of problem solving has six steps:

1. Locate and define the problem.
2. List the causes of the problem.
3. List possible solutions.
4. Discuss the advantages and disadvantages of each solution.
5. Choose the best solution.
6. Decide how to put that solution into effect.

The following exercise may be done individually or as a group project:

What is the problem to be solved? _____

_____

Define any special or confusing terms. _____

_____

What are the causes of the problem? _____

_____

What are possible solutions to the problem?

1. _____

2. _____

3. _____

4. _____

After discussing the advantages and disadvantages of each solution, choose the best one.

Solution chosen: _____

After discussing the way to put the solution into effect, list the method to be used:

_____

Name _____ Date _____

Group Presentation: A Round Table

1. Form a group for the discussion.
2. Select a topic to discuss.
3. Choose a discussion leader.
4. Choose a group recorder and a flow sheet recorder.
5. Determine the time limitations for the discussion.
6. If the topic is such that research would be beneficial, have each group member research an aspect of the topic.
7. The group leader should keep the discussion moving along and on track.
8. During the discussion, the recorder should make notes of the major points of the discussion. The flow sheet recorder should make a list of the names of the participants and mark behind each name every time the person adds to the discussion. The teacher may collect both reports at the end of the discussion.

Group Presentation: A Panel

Follow the first seven steps listed for a round table discussion. Instead of step eight in the list for a round table discussion, give each member of the audience a copy of the rating sheet for a discussion group (page 66) to fill out.

Group Presentation: A Symposium

1. Form the group for the symposium.
2. Select a topic to discuss.
3. Determine the time limit for each presentation.
4. Choose a member of the group to be the moderator and make introductions.
5. Each member of the discussion group should choose an aspect of the topic.
6. The members should then research the topic.
7. The moderator should give an opening statement to the audience about the topic. He or she should then introduce the first member of the group and the aspect of the topic that member will present. The moderator then introduces each additional member. At the conclusion of the last presentation, the moderator should present concluding remarks.

Name _____ Date _____

Discussion: Rating Sheet

The audience members should fill out a flow chart as the discussion occurs. They should fill out the rating section after the discussion.

Type of discussion group: _____

Topic of the discussion: _____

Flow Sheet

On the back of this page, list the name of each member of the discussion. Each time a group member speaks, put a mark after his or her name. (This means each separate time each speaks, not how long they speak.)

Rating

Rate the speech on each of the following points, using this scale:

1 – poor   2 – average   3 – good   4 – very good   5 – excellent

_____ Were the participants well prepared?

_____ Did everyone participate in the discussion? (Check the flow sheet.)

_____ Were the major points clear?

_____ Were the major points well supported?

_____ Did the discussion move along well?

_____ How well did the group work together?

_____ Did the discussion keep my attention and interest?

_____ Did the members of the group speak loudly enough to be heard?

_____ Did the members of the group speak clearly?

_____ **TOTAL POINTS**

Debate

Debating is the most complex and difficult type of spoken communication. A *debate* is a discussion of two opposing views of a topic. Everyone has had many informal debates. They are a means of solving problems. Debates occur at home as well as at town meetings, state legislatures, Congress, and courtrooms.

Debating helps develop many speaking skills, as well as a variety of other skills. Debaters become better informed on current events. They develop reasoning, critical thinking, and researching abilities. They also learn how to think quickly and respond under pressure.

Formal debates have special rules and time limits agreed to in advance. Most formal debates occur in high schools and colleges throughout the world.

Each formal debate has a proposition. The *proposition* states the conflict in a sentence that can be answered "yes" or "no." An example of a debate proposition is "Resolved: That the United States increase spending on education." A debate proposition usually suggests a change. The proposition cannot be one-sided. Speakers must be able to defend realistically either side of the proposition.

A formal debate has two teams. Each team usually has two members who work together. The Lincoln-Douglas format only uses one member on each team. The *affirmative team* is for the change in the proposition. The *negative team* is against the change. They are for the *status quo,* which means the way the things are at present.

The members of each team then do research on the proposition topic. They search for proof and evidence that their side has the best answer. They must be able to give the reasons for supporting their side. They must also show support for their reasons.

A formal debate has a predetermined order of speeches. It also has strict time limits for each speaker. Debates usually have timekeepers. The timekeeper calls out when the speaker has reached his or her time limit. The speaker must stop immediately when the timekeeper announces that time has run out. Time limits are important so that neither side has the advantage of extra time.

Each member of the team presents material to support their side during the first part of a debate. They give as much proof as possible during their opening speech.

The latter part of a debate is the *rebuttal.* During the rebuttal times each speaker has the opportunity to answer questions and respond to points raised by the other side.

A team member may speak only during his or her turn. Members may not interrupt the speaker for any reason. Each member may ask questions at any time during his or her turn, but the other team may not respond until it is their turn to speak.

Formal debates have three common formats: the *standard format,* the *cross-examination format,* and the *Lincoln-Douglas format.* The speaking time for each format varies.

Debates, unlike most communication, are win or lose situations. Most debates are judged. The judge or judges decide which side has done the best job of stating their position, giving evidence to support their views, and responding to the questions of the other team.

Debate Formats

Time limits differ according to the total time available for the debate. The times listed on these charts are typical.

The Standard Debate Format

1st Affirmative	10 minutes
1st Negative	10 minutes
2nd Affirmative	10 minutes
2nd Negative	10 minutes
1st Negative rebuttal	5 minutes
1st Affirmative rebuttal	5 minutes
2nd Negative rebuttal	5 minutes
2nd Affirmative rebuttal	5 minutes

The Cross-Examination Format

1st Affirmative	8 minutes
1st Negative cross-examines	3 minutes
1st Negative	8 minutes
2nd Affirmative cross-examines	3 minutes
2nd Affirmative	8 minutes
2nd Negative cross-examines	3 minutes
2nd Negative	8 minutes
1st Affirmative cross-examines	3 minutes
1st Negative rebuttal	4 minutes
1st Affirmative rebuttal	4 minutes
2nd Negative rebuttal	4 minutes
2nd Affirmative rebuttal	4 minutes

Notice that the affirmative has the slight advantage of speaking both first and last in the presentation.

The Lincoln-Douglas Format

(This format uses only two speakers.)

Affirmative speech	6 minutes
Negative cross-examination	3 minutes
Negative speech	7 minutes
Affirmative cross-examination	3 minutes
Affirmative rebuttal	4 minutes
Negative rebuttal	6 minutes
Affirmative rebuttal	3 minutes

Notice that the affirmative speaker gets to speak once more often, but both speakers have the same amount of total time.

Name _____ Date _____

Questions for Consideration

1. What is a debate?

_____

2. How is a formal debate different from an informal debate?

_____

3. Where do most formal debates happen?

_____

4. How must a debate proposition be able to be answered?

_____

5. How many teams are in a debate?

_____

6. Usually, how many members are on each team?

_____

7. What are the names of the two teams?

_____

8. Which team is in favor of a change?

_____

9. What is the status quo?

_____

10. Why are time limits in a debate important?

_____

11. What is the latter part of a debate called?

_____

12. When is the only time a team member may speak?

_____

13. What are the three common debate formats?

_____

_____

Name _____ Date _____

Debate: Vocabulary

The following is a list of words used in the narrative about debate. Look each of them up in a dictionary and copy the meaning on this sheet. After the meaning, write a sentence using the word appropriately, or give an example of the word.

1. Reasoning _____

_____

2. Formal _____

_____

3. Proposition _____

_____

4. Affirmative _____

_____

5. Negative _____

_____

6. Status quo _____

_____

7. Rebuttal _____

_____

8. Cross-examination _____

_____

9. Current events _____

_____

10. Format _____

_____

Name _____ Date _____

Group Presentation: A Debate

1. Decide on the type of debate format to use. Also decide on the time limits.
2. Select the topic and write the proposition. Remember the topic must have two defendable sides and be written to propose a change.
3. Select the team members and decide who will be on the affirmative and who will be on the negative team. Also decide who will be first and second speaker on each team.
4. Select the day for the debate and choose a timekeeper.
5. Have the team members research the topic and begin building their cases and organizing the evidence.
6. Present the debate at the scheduled time. The judge and perhaps members of the audience should fill out the rating sheet for the debate.

Debate proposition: Resolved: _____

Debate format to be used: _____

Timekeeper: _____

Time limits: _____   _____

                        _____   _____

                        _____   _____

                        _____   _____

                        _____   _____

                        _____   _____

                        _____   _____

Team Members:

First Affirmative: _____

Second Affirmative: _____

First Negative: _____

Second Negative: _____

Name _____ Date _____

Rating Sheet for a Debate

PROPOSITION: _____

Rate each area with: 1 – poor   2 – average   3 – good   4 – very good   5 – excellent

FIRST AFFIRMATIVE

Name _____

Opening

_____ Was well prepared

_____ Presented strong arguments

_____ Used evidence effectively

_____ Asked good questions

Rebuttal (or cross-examination)

_____ Answered questions well

_____ Defended the side appropriately

_____ Overall presentation (speaking voice, posture, eye contact, and so on)

_____ TOTAL POINTS

_____ TOTAL TEAM POINTS

    (add the scores of both team members)

SECOND AFFIRMATIVE

Name _____

Opening

_____ Was well prepared

_____ Presented strong arguments

_____ Used evidence effectively

_____ Asked good questions

Rebuttal (or cross-examination)

_____ Answered questions well

_____ Defended the side appropriately

_____ Overall presentation (speaking voice, posture, eye contact, and so on)

_____ TOTAL POINTS

FIRST NEGATIVE

Name _____

Opening

_____ Was well prepared

_____ Presented strong arguments

_____ Used evidence effectively

_____ Asked good questions

Rebuttal (or cross-examination)

_____ Answered questions well

_____ Defended the side appropriately

_____ Overall presentation (speaking voice, posture, eye contact, and so on)

_____ TOTAL POINTS

_____ TOTAL TEAM POINTS

    (add the scores of both team members)

SECOND NEGATIVE

Name _____

Opening

_____ Was well prepared

_____ Presented strong arguments

_____ Used evidence effectively

_____ Asked good questions

Rebuttal (or cross-examination)

_____ Answered questions well

_____ Defended the side appropriately

_____ Overall presentation (speaking voice, posture, eye contact, and so on)

_____ TOTAL POINTS

Oral Interpretation

Oral interpretation is the reading out loud of literature. It is an interesting and rewarding method of presentation. Oral interpretation performances include poetry, prose, and drama. Many high schools have oral interpretation presentations as part of their contest speech work.

Many people use oral interpretation every day. All of these are examples of using oral interpretation: a parent reading a story to a child, a news commentator reporting the latest happenings, a teacher reading to a class, and a minister reading from a text.

The performers of oral interpretation do not move around the stage area. They do not use costumes, props, scenery, or stage make-up. They are readers, not actors. They rely only on the sound of their voices saying the words of the text.

Oral interpretation readers analyze the words of the text. They then mark the words to help them remember how to use their voices when reading aloud.

The human voice becomes the focus of the presentation. Readers use extra work and effort to make the sound of their voices as interesting and full of expression as possible. The key to having good expression is variety. Without variety, the voice becomes monotonous and boring. Most people do not use the full variety available in their voices when speaking every day. Good readers, speakers, and performers add variety to their voices in several ways.

Pitch is how high or low the voice sounds. When we are nervous or excited, we use a higher pitched voice. We use lower pitches when we are relaxed or sad.

Volume is how loudly a person speaks. People are louder when they are angry or forceful. They speak softly when they are sad or romantic. The performer must remember that even when they are speaking softly to get the proper effect, they still must be loud enough for the audience to hear every word.

Inflection is the changing of pitch within a sentence. Questions often end with a rising inflection. Statements of fact end with a lower inflection. Speakers can obtain variety by changing inflection within a sentence.

Rhythm is a regular reoccurring flow of sound and silence. It is also the pattern of stressed and unstressed syllables in a sentence. We are more familiar with rhythm in music than we are in speaking. We speak with faster rhythms when we are excited or frightened. We use slower rhythms when we are tired or bored.

Meter is most often important in reading poetry. It is the count of syllables in a line.

Quality refers to the overall sound of the voice. A voice with good quality has a full, rich sound. Speakers can improve voice quality with effort and practice. A voice is said to be nasal when too much sound is forced through the nose and upper part of the throat. One way to improve the quality of the voice is to open the mouth wider while speaking. This allows more sound through the mouth rather than the nose.

Name _____ Date _____

Questions for Consideration

1. What is oral interpretation?

_____

2. What do the performers rely on most when doing an oral interpretation reading?

_____

3. What is the key to good vocal expression?

_____

4. What is pitch?

_____

5. What usually happens to the pitch of a voice when a person is nervous?

_____

6. What usually happens to the voice's volume when someone is angry?

_____

7. What must the performer always remember about volume when reading aloud?

_____

8. What is inflection?

_____

9. What usually ends with a rising inflection?

_____

10. What two things did the narrative mention as part of rhythm?

_____

_____

11. What is meter?

_____

12. When is attention to meter most important?

_____

13. What is quality when referring to the voice?

_____

Name _____ Date _____

Presentations: Oral Interpretation

We express a great deal of meaning by the way we use our voices in addition to the meaning of the words we use. These exercises will help develop better vocal expression.

Reading nonsense: Write a list of fifty words that do not make sense or do not give any message when used together. Examples include names from a phone book, a list of ingredients in a recipe, a paragraph read backwards, and so forth. Practice reading the list aloud in the following ways: happy, sad, angry, silly, powerful, and weak. As you read the list, use variety in the voice to express the feeling. Do not rely on the meaning of the words.

Change emphasis: Say the following sentence several times: "I didn't know she was the one who ate the cake." Each time you say the sentence, emphasize a different word. Notice how the meaning of the sentence changes just by having a different word emphasized.

Tongue twisters: Tongue twisters are sentences that are difficult to say clearly. They are good for practicing speaking clearly. Practice the following sentences until you can say them quickly:

Peter Piper picked a peck of pickled peppers.

Does this shop stock short socks with spots?

How much wood could a woodchuck chuck, if a woodchuck could chuck wood?

Silly Simon sifted a sieve full of unsifted thistles.

Next, write and practice three of your own tongue twisters.

Reading a poem: Find a poem of about twelve or fourteen lines. Read it repeatedly until you are familiar with it. Look up any words that are not familiar. Write it out on a piece of paper. Leave extra space between each of the lines. To help analyze the selection, mark the following:

Pay attention to the punctuation. Pauses and inflection depend on punctuation, not just the end of the line of written words. (Some readers write a poem as if it were prose, written in paragraph form, to help with understanding.) Underline each comma once, any colons or semi-colons twice, periods and question marks three times, and any exclamation points four times. These marks indicate how much emphasis to give in pausing or power for each mark. Emphasize a comma (one underline) less than a period (three underlines).

Circle all key words. Circle the most important word in each line or phrase.

Use an arrow pointing up when you want to increase the volume or raise the pitch of the voice. Use an arrow pointing down when you want to decrease the volume or lower the pitch of the voice.

Put a wavy line under any special sounding words, such as words that the sound itself helps give meaning.

Practice reading the selection using these notations until you are comfortable enough to read the poem aloud to an audience.

Name _____ Date _____

Oral Interpretation: Crossword Puzzle

Use the clues below to complete the crossword puzzle. Answers to the questions can be found in the narrative dealing with oral interpretation.

ACROSS

3. People doing oral interpretation are this, not actors.
9. In poetry, the count of syllables in a line
10. The loudness of the voice
12. When too much sound comes through the nose
13. The high or low sound of the voice
14. Performers add _____ to their voices in several ways.
15. The reading out loud of literature (two words)

DOWN

1. Performers of oral interpretation do not use _____ or props.
2. Oral interpretation includes reading poetry, _____ , and drama.
4. Readers try to make the sound of their voices as interesting and full of _____ as possible.
5. The pattern of stressed and unstressed syllables in a sentence
6. The changing of pitch within a sentence
7. The overall sound of the voice
8. Without variety, the voice becomes boring and _____ .
11. The human _____ becomes the focus of attention when reading aloud.

Pantomime

Pantomime is communicating without using words. The performer uses his or her face, hands, and body posture instead of words to give a message to the audience. Gestures and facial expressions become quite important in this form of communication. A mime can communicate an idea, a feeling, or a story.

The words *mime* and *pantomime* mean the same thing to most people. However, some individuals use the two words differently. They believe mime requires greater skill and training than pantomime. During Christmas time in Great Britain, some theaters present pantomimes, called *pantos*. *Pantos* are productions of children's stories. The pantos are not truly pantomimes since they use spoken words.

Many people refer to mime as an international art since it does not use words. People throughout the world understand mime instantly. It does not need any translation into another language.

Mime artists seldom use any objects in their work. Through their movements and gestures they show the imaginary object.

Actors sometimes use mime as part of a regular performance. They do this to communicate in addition to the spoken words used. Entire presentations using just mime are also popular.

Many actors study mime to help them relax physically during a performance. Mime helps them to gain better control over the parts of their bodies. Mime techniques aid actors in moving and gesturing while performing. It also helps actors to appear more natural on stage.

No one knows when mime began. We assume that primitive people used mime to tell stories around the campfire. Mime was an important part of theater in the ancient Greek and Roman times. It continued to be popular in the 1700s and 1800s. *Commedia dell' arte* was a popular form of Italian comedy that used a great deal of mime.

The silent movies also used a great deal of mime. Charlie Chaplin, Buster Keaton, Laurel and Hardy, and other early film actors were excellent mime artists. Mime is still a popular form of entertainment. Other noted twentieth century mimes include Etienne Decroux, Jean-Louis Barrault, Marcel Marceau, Shields and Yarnell, and Richmond Shepard.

Most pantomimes are *stylized.* This means that they are not just an exact reproduction of something. They take the basis of something, then clarify and enlarge it. Mimes first learn how to control and use the body for maximum expression. They have many exercises to develop movement, posture, and the use of gestures. The mime then learns to simplify and clarify an action. A mime will refine a process or emotion to just the basics of physical movement. A mime eliminates any unneeded movement. This helps the audience understand and appreciate the meaning more easily. The mime may also enlarge and perhaps exaggerate the movements for the audience in the back of the room to see more clearly.

Name _____ Date _____

Questions for Consideration

1. What is pantomime?

_____

2. What three things do mimes use instead of words to communicate?

_____

3. What is the difference between mime and pantomime to most people?

_____

4. What two things do some people consider to be more necessary in mime than pantomime?

_____

5. What are British Christmas presentations of children's stories called?

_____

6. Why are they not true pantomimes?

_____

7. Why is mime called an international art?

_____

_____

8. What four things does the study of mime do for actors?

_____

_____

_____

_____

9. What was the name of Italian comedy that used mime?

_____

10. Who were two famous silent film mimes that were mentioned in the narrative?

_____

Name _____ Date _____

Presentations: Mime

Below are listed some basic mime exercises. They include projects for individuals, partnerships, and small group work.

Discovering an object: Mime the following action: Walk down the street. See something on the pavement. Look at the object. Mime picking the object up. Show what the object looks like by handling it. How heavy is it? What is its shape? How large is it? Now use the object as it is intended. For example: If the object is a ball, you could show that it is round by how you mimed picking it up. Your hands would be curved. You would show how large it is by whether you used one or two hands to pick it up. The size of a larger ball is indicated by the distance between your hands as you pick it up. You could mime using the ball by tossing it in the air and catching it, or bouncing it on the ground.

Define a box: Another popular mime exercise is to define the sides and top of a box. Pretend that you are in a large invisible box. Move around in the box until you reach one side of it. Show that you have reached the side. Show that it is a flat surface by touching it with your hands. Move along the side until you reach the corner. Show by using your hands that it is a square corner, then show the next wall. Continue the exercise until you show all four sides and the top of the box.

Doing a process: Select a common task to perform. For example: get ready for school, pour and drink a glass of water, or make a salad. Perform the actual task. As you are doing the task, concentrate on every movement you make. Next, mime doing the task. Do not use any real objects. Try to recreate the process as accurately as you can.

A mirror image: Choose a partner. Have one person perform a common task that has more than one part in the process. For example: brush your teeth and comb your hair. The partner pretends to be a mirror and does the same task at the same time. The object is for both partners to move and do the task at exactly the same time. The first person should make all movements slowly and clearly. The task is not to trick or fool your partner. Remember, a mirror gives a reverse image. If the first person uses his or her right hand, the partner will need to use the left hand. After doing the exercise until it becomes natural, reverse roles and have the first person become the mirror.

A group activity: Have one member of the group perform a task. The other members of the group then join in one at a time. They help the first person with the task or do a related part of the task. Continue the activity until all members of the group become involved. Remember not to use any words during the exercise. For example: the first person may mime mowing a lawn; as others join in, one person might trim a hedge, another might rake the grass clippings, another person could bag the clippings, someone else might sweep the sidewalk, and so forth.

79

Improvisation

Improvisation (or an improv) is an exciting and fun activity. Actors often practice it to sharpen their performance skills. Rehearsals, and at times performances, often include improvs.

Improvisation is a form of the word improvise. To improvise is to make something up. *Theatrical improv* is making up the story and acting it out at the same time. It includes making up the characters, location, situation, events, movements, and words spoken.

Improvs help the actor think quickly and make interesting dramatic choices. They also help encourage creativity and develop concentration. Improvs also develop trust and teamwork within a group.

Teachers often use improvs as exercises or practice for building skills. He or she guides the group through the project and often gives the beginning situation. The teacher also *coaches,* or gives helpful suggestions, as the improvisation continues. The teacher may also add information or change the direction of the improvisation by changing some information. The teacher usually decides when to end the improv.

Improvs can also become public performances. The cast rehearses together before the performance. This helps them to get used to working as a team. They usually know the outline of action, but they present the performance fresh for the first time. Sometimes, the performers ask members of the audience for suggestions. The performers then work these suggestions into the improv.

Some improvs begin with no preplanning. Two or more performers get together and begin to make up the presentation.

Most improvs have a starting situation. They may also have characters decided upon in advance. For example: a customer wants to return some merchandise but the salesperson does not want to accept it, or some friends are planning a social event, but they cannot agree on what they want to do.

Many improvs use an outline. The outline is simple and contains just the major events that will happen. Most outlines include the beginning situation, three or four major events, and the conclusion. The performers memorize the outline and then begin the improvisation. The performers should avoid overplanning and overpreparation. The improv must remain new and fresh. An improv does not need to include a conflict. However, having the improv about a conflict, or adding a conflict to it will help make it more interesting.

It is helpful to remember that an improv is not a competition. It requires good teamwork. Each member of the team must contribute to the improv and encourage the other members during the activity. Each member must use his or her imagination without fear of failure. It is important to say and do things that another teammate can build upon. All members should avoid negative words and actions. A team member should never become embarrassed or discouraged by attempting to participate.

Performers should attempt to have things they say or do add to the progress of the improv. They should try to make everything realistic in the situation. They should not do anything that their character would be unlikely to do. The performers should try to have everything they do move the story along.

80

Name _____ Date _____

Questions for Consideration

1. Why do actors practice improvisations?

_____

2. What are three things that improvisations can help an actor do?

_____

_____

3. Name three things a teacher does when a class does an improv.

_____

_____

_____

4. Why do cast members of a publicly presented improvisation rehearse?

_____

5. What do audience members sometimes provide for an improvisation?

_____

6. What do improvisation cast members usually do with an outline before a performance?

_____

7. What two things must improvisation cast members avoid doing?

_____

8. What will often make an improvisation more interesting?

_____

9. What are five things that a team member should remember when doing an improv?

_____

_____

_____

Name _____ Date _____

Presentations: Improvisation

Two Person Exercises

Working out a conflict: Select two team members. Choose a topic that has a conflict. Have each member argue for one side of the conflict. Possible topics include:

- One student wants to copy another student's answer sheet for a homework assignment. The other student does not want his or her answers copied.
- A young person wants to borrow the car. The parent does not want the car driven.
- Two friends try to decide what to do for fun. One wants to go to a movie, the other wants to go to the mall.

Finishing a sentence: The team chooses a task that requires giving directions. One person begins a sentence. The other person then finishes the sentence. This continues until the team completes giving the directions.

Group Exercises

A group effort: Have the group choose an activity that requires teamwork. One member of the group begins the activity. The other members of the group join in the activity one at a time.

On the job: The team chooses a work place. Each member chooses a character. The group then improvises a few minutes on the job. One group member could be the boss. Other members portray workers. Some team members may portray customers if appropriate to the situation.

Telling a story: Have the members of the group form a circle looking at each other. The first person begins to tell the story by saying the first three words. Going around the circle, each person adds the next three words. Keep going around the circle until the team completes the story.

Using suggestions: Have each member of the group write the following suggested items, each on a separate piece of paper: a location or setting, an important topic, a character type, a job or profession, and a conflict. Put the pieces of paper in separate piles, one for each of the responses. Divide the group into groups of five or six members. Every member of the group chooses one sheet of paper from the character and job papers. Each will portray that character and worker. One member from each group chooses one sheet of paper from the location, topic, and conflict suggestion sheets.

Each group then does an improvisation based on the suggestions written on the papers they chose.

Writing a Play

Writing a play is a rewarding experience. It is also a more difficult task than most people realize. The person who writes the play is a *playwright.* Notice that the spelling of the word ends with "wright," not "write." The word *wright* means one who forms or makes something. The words used to describe the process of creating a play are *play writing.* Notice that this phrase ends with "writing," not "wrighting."

Plays come in all lengths and styles. Some are only one act and can be quite short. One-act plays usually take between 15 minutes to one hour to perform. Full-length plays usually last between one to three hours. Most modern playwrights write in prose. However, some playwrights use poetry for their plays. Plays can deal with any subject. Most are realistic, but many fantasy plays exist. Plays use the full range of human emotions. They may be funny, sad, thrilling, or inspiring.

Writing a play is different from writing a short story or novel. A writer describes things and tells about them. In a play, the audience sees things, so they do not have to be described. A playwright *shows* things happening, rather than telling about them. A playwright uses many literary devices to do his work. Some of the more important tools are explained in the rest of this narrative.

Plot is the story of the play. It is the series of events that happen. These events should be interesting.

The word *character* refers to the people in the play. Character descriptions can answer many important questions. What are they like? What makes them special or different? How are they related? Why do they do what they do?

Theme is the meaning or message of the play. Some plays have a special meaning in addition to just what happens in the plot. Many plays contain something important to teach the audience.

The *setting* of the play is when and where it happens. The most obvious part of setting is the space in which the play takes place. Some settings include places such as a living room, a street, or an office. Additional parts of the setting may include in what city or country the play is set. The time of the play may also be important. The year, the time of day, or the season may be of importance.

Dialogue refers to the words spoken by the characters in the play. The actors' dialogue is often referred to as their "lines."

It is very important that *action* takes place in a play. If the play only has characters talking about something happening, the play can be quite dull. It is better to show action on stage than to just talk about it.

Every good play contains *conflict.* Many times two or more characters want different things and this causes the conflict. Another common source of conflict is when a major character wants something, but objects stand in the way.

Name _____ Date _____

Questions for Consideration

1. What is a person who writes plays called?

_____

2. What is the process of writing a play called?

_____

3. How long are most one-act plays?

_____

4. What does a writer of plays do instead of describing something?

_____

5. What word describes the telling of the events that happen in a play?

_____

6. What word refers to the people in a play?

_____

7. What word refers to the meaning or message of a play?

_____

8. What word describes where and when the play takes place?

_____

9. What, in addition to the location, may be included in the word from question #8?

_____

_____

10. What word refers to the words spoken by the characters in a play?

_____

11. What is another word used to describe the actors' speeches?

_____

12. What word describes the events that happen in a play, rather than those just talked about?

_____

13. What happens between the characters that is necessary for a good play?

_____

Name _____ Date _____

Getting an Idea

Getting an idea for a play is often difficult. At other times, an idea will come into the playwright's mind immediately. Ideas for a play can come from a variety of sources. This exercise may help you to find an idea for a play that you will find exciting and fun.

What's in the news? Many good subjects for a play appear in newspapers or magazines every day. The story does not have to be one of the major stories. Perhaps a smaller story would be better. The finished play does not have to tell the exact story. The story may just give an idea to help start the play. Look through a few issues of a newspaper or magazine. Find four stories that could be used to write your play. On the blanks below, write a brief sentence giving the basic idea from each story.

1. _____

_____

2. _____

_____

3. _____

_____

4. _____

_____

Whom do you remember? Many plays develop out of characters. List four of the most interesting or unusual people you have known. After each name, tell what you remember about them that makes them interesting or unique.

1. _____

_____

2. _____

_____

3. _____

_____

4. _____

_____

Name _____ Date _____

Getting an Idea (continued)

What has happened to you or a friend? Many plays are biographical. List four interesting or unusual things that have happened to you or a friend that would be good stories to tell others.

1. _____

_____

2. _____

_____

3. _____

_____

4. _____

_____

What subject is interesting to you? Another source of ideas for a play can come from a special interest you already have. If something is of interest to you, it should be easier for you to share it with others. List four special interests you have.

1. _____

_____

2. _____

_____

3. _____

_____

4. _____

_____

After completing this exercise, you should have a list of 16 possible ideas that you might want to use for your play. Look over this list, and then choose one that is your favorite.

My choice is _____

_____

Name _____ Date _____

Exploring Setting and Character

This exercise will help explore the setting and characters for your play. Use the idea that you chose as your favorite from Getting an Idea to complete this exercise.

What is the idea that you have chosen to use for your play? _____
_____

Setting: What are the parts of the setting for this play? _____
_____

    Where will the play take place? _____
    In what city and country? _____
    In what year? _____ What time of day? _____
    In what season? _____
    How much time will pass during the play? _____

Character: The main character in a play is the *protagonist.* The major character who is opposed to the protagonist is the *antagonist.* The two characters provide the conflict necessary for a good play.

Who is the protagonist in the play? _____
    What is this character's main goal? _____
    List four things about this character that will be important in the play:
        1. _____
        2. _____
        3. _____
        4. _____

Who is the main antagonist in the play? _____
    What is this character's main goal? _____
    What is the relationship between the protagonist and the antagonist? _____
_____
    List four things about this character that will be important in the play.
        1. _____
        2. _____
        3. _____
        4. _____

Name _____ Date _____

Outlining the Plot

Most plots contain a structure similar to this:

The following outline may help you write the play. The outline should be an aid but shoul not limit you. Do not worry if things do not end up as you outlined them. Do not be afraid to make changes. Be flexible.

I. EXPOSITION. The exposition consists of the most important things that the audience must learn before they can understand and follow the action of the rest of the play. List four parts of the exposition for your play.

   A. _____
   B. _____
   C. _____
   D. _____

II. TURNING POINT. The turning point is the important thing that happens to change the direction of the play. Something happens that changes the lives of the characters and their relationships to each other. What will be the turning point of your play?

   A. _____

III. RISING ACTION. The rising action consists of events that happen after the turning point. They move the play along until the climax is reached. Good rising action keeps building interest and excitement in the play. List four important things that would be rising action in your play.

   A. _____
   B. _____
   C. _____
   D. _____

IV. CLIMAX. The climax is the most important thing that happens in the play. What is the climax of your play?

   A. _____

V. RESOLUTION. The resolution is what happens after the climax. What are the major changes that happen because of the climax?

   A. _____
   B. _____

Name _____ Date _____

Writing Your Play

You are now ready to write your play. Plays are written in a special format. Here are some suggestions.

The first page is a title page. It is very simple. The title page should include the title of the play. This is centered on the page, both from side to side as well as from the top to bottom of the page.

The second page usually contains the list of characters. Each character's name is followed by a brief description of the character. For example:

MELISSA JONES..... A pretty girl. She is twenty years old. She is a talented dancer.
HEATHER JONES...MELISSA's younger sister. She is nineteen years old and only
    interested in boys. She likes to tease her older sister.

The second page often includes the setting. For example:

The Scene: Act I: The living room of the Jones' house. It is fall 1996.
              Act II: The same, one week later.

The third page is often the first page of the actual play. The character's name is followed by a colon. The lines that the character says follow. Any special directions for the character are put inside parentheses. An extra line is left to separate lines said by the different characters. For example:

MELISSA: I wonder where Uncle Mike is. He usually isn't this late.

HEATHER: You know how forgetful he is. He may not remember that it's your
            birthday today.

MELISSA: He'd better not forget. (She looks out of the window.) I think he almost
            forgot about it last year.

HEATHER: (sadly) I wonder why he is getting so forgetful.

Go ahead and write your play. Good luck! Here are some additional hints:

• Do not expect to get everything right the first time. Most playwrights rewrite many times
  to get things exactly as they want them.
• Do not be surprised if your characters seem to say things, or go in a direction that you did
  not plan. They may almost seem to have lives of their own.
• Do not be surprised if you get stuck and don't know what to write next. This is called writer's
  block and is quite common. Keep trying, or do something else for a while and then come
  back to the project.
• It is sometimes helpful to read aloud what you have written. Perhaps someone will be
  willing to read your play to you. Remember, plays are to be seen and heard, not just read.

Answer Keys

Communication (page 3)
1. the transfer of meaning
2. sender, receiver, message, medium
3. media
4. mass media
5. non-verbal
6. verbal
7. interpersonal
8. discussion
9. public
10. The actor pretends to be someone else.
11. study and practice and continue to learn

Communication: Crossword (page 5)

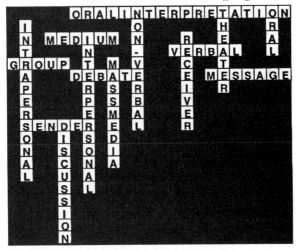

Stage Fright (page 7)
1. fear of appearing on stage
2. realize how common it is
3. butterflies in the stomach
4. upset stomach, perspiration, trembling, dry or wet mouth (any three)
5. everyone has stage fright
6. adrenaline
7. Stage fright is nature's way of helping face a challenge.
8. gain experience, prepare well, realize it is natural, realize the audience wants success, realize the audience is not the enemy, relax physically (any four)
9. Things can be done to lessen stage fright.
10. the speaker

Interviewing (page 10)
1. the person doing the interview
2. the person being interviewed
3. one-on-one
4. job interview
5. gather information
6. any three: keep on the right track, get started, keep moving smoothly, prompt memory
7. discuss more thoroughly
8. those that can be answered by just "yes" or "no"
9. too many
10. taken neatly and carefully (or clear and understandable)
11. soon
12. get permission to use it

Preparing to Give a Speech (page 15)
1. use proper presentation skills
2. audience and occasion
3. get the audience's attention
4. concise, well organized
5. speaking loudly and clearly
6. speaking clearly
7. d, t, ing
8. variety of pitch
9. a question
10. It becomes monotonous.
11. with weight on both feet
12. helps to appear more involved
13. sounds or words that creep into the speech such as "ah" or "you know"

Preparing to Give a Speech: Word Search (page 16)

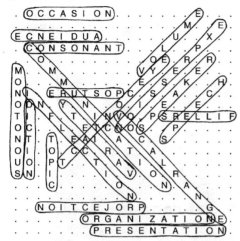

Methods of Organization: Word Search (page 25)

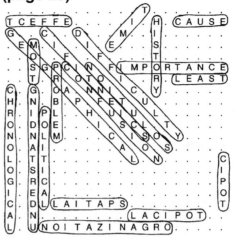

Choosing a Topic (page 18)
1. makes the rest of the task easier
2. creates extra work and difficulty
3. find something already of interest
4. your enthusiasm can spread
5. give the speaker an idea for a topic
6. answers vary
7. make a list of topics, evaluate each
8. answers vary
9. narrow the topic

Methods of Organization (page 22)
1. follow what the speaker has to say
2. confusion
3. chronological
4. describing a process or history
5. spatial
6. least to most important, most to least important
7. cause and effect
8. problem to solution
9. difficulty
10. least to most difficult, most to least difficult
11. topical

The Introduction of a Speech (page 27)
1. get the audience's attention, introduce the topic, and provide smooth movement to the rest of the speech
2. first impressions
3. attention device
4. makes them want to listen
5. humor, interesting story, surprising or curious fact
6. the preview
7. giving a definition, explanation
8. movement from one part to the next
9. one sentence
10. write it down
11. the speech seems rough or choppy

The Body of a Speech (page 30)
1. it will lack depth
2. It will be difficult for the audience to remember them all.
3. three or four
4. order of importance, chronological order, space order, problem to solution, cause and effect (any four)
5. words to help guide the audience through the speech
6. of equal importance
7. help the audience understand and remember
8. definitions, examples, facts

9. outlining the speech
10. realize the proper emphasis and show where supporting material is needed

The Conclusion of a Speech (page 34)
1. transition, good final statement
2. review
3. transition
4. three
5. preview in the introduction, in the body, and in the review in the conclusion
6. clincher, wrap up, oomph statement
7. the audience does not know the speaker is finished
8. statement or fact, interesting question, challenge to the audience, joke or story
9. "Now you know about. . . " and "Are there any questions?"

Presenting Information (page 37)
1. informative
2. should be in greater detail or depth
3. introduction, body, conclusion
4. trying to give too much information
5. the audience's attention
6. arranging material to keep building interest, and relating the topic to the audience
7. giving information, then strengthening it
8. use visual aids, restate in other words, use an example, give a comparison (any two)
9. something seen by the audience
10. It is less distracting.

Using Supporting Materials (page 40)
1. better understand the material, have confidence in the speaker
2. a good source
3. facts
4. information presented as numbers
5. parts of the whole
6. a new, unclear, or specialized word
7. the exact words
8. similarities
9. differences
10. similes, metaphors, analogies

11. saying something again using other words
12. two or three

Using Supporting Materials: Crossword Puzzle (page 42)

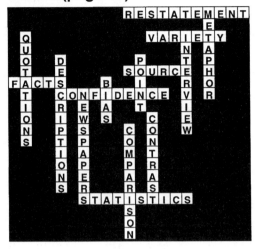

Persuasion (page 44)
1. help us persuade others, help us make better decisions
2. change beliefs, attitudes, or behavior
3. to get the audience to do something
4. purpose, topic
5. Who is the audience? What do they believe?
6. to get them involved
7. becoming what one wishes to be
8. self-esteem
9. food, clothing, shelter, fresh air, water
10. specific
11. knows the topic, is honest, and is sincere

Using Visual Aids (page 49)
1. things shown to the audience
2. assist the audience in understanding
3. visual, something to see
4. the speech
5. they must be visible to the entire audience
6. the size of the audience and room
7. to the side of or behind the aid
8. the aid may get damaged, may take focus from the speaker
9. at the time when it illustrates the point
10. It should be clean, neat, and attractive.

11. It may become cluttered and confusing.
12. to lessen the chance of an error

Doing a Demonstration (page 52)
1. a speech to inform
2. shows it
3. steps in a process
4. chronological
5. hearing and seeing
6. on the visual aid
7. the visual aid prompts memory
8. whatever the audience sees
9. help communicate effectively
10. too simple or too complex
11. standing in front of the aid
12. to lessen the chance of it not working
13. a back-up plan

Special Occasion Speeches (page 56)
1. honor persons, celebrate special achievements or events (some students may list honor, inspire, challenge)
2. get the audience's attention and get the audience interested in the topic
3. background, why speaker is an authority on topic
4. description of award, reason person is receiving it
5. short
6. listing too many
7. speech to honor someone no longer living
8. speech that remembers a special event
9. inspires, challenges
10. why the subject is important to them

Discussion (page 62)
1. interpersonal
2. dialogue
3. group discussion
4. share views, hear other's views
5. cooperation
6. a common purpose
7. keep discussion moving in an orderly way
8. give everyone an equal chance to participate

9. small group of people chosen from a larger group
10. group discussion for benefit of the participants
11. group discussion for benefit of an audience
12. group presentation to audience; includes prepared speeches
13. round table

Discussion: Word Search (page 63)

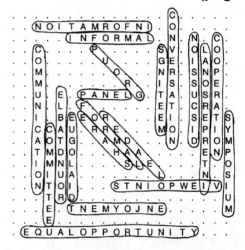

Debate (page 69)
1. a discussion of two opposing views of a topic
2. they have rules and time limits
3. in high schools and colleges
4. "yes" or "no"
5. two
6. two
7. affirmative, negative
8. affirmative
9. the way things are
10. so that neither side has an advantage
11. rebuttal
12. during their turn
13. standard, cross-examination, Lincoln-Douglas

Oral Interpretation (page 74)

1. the reading out loud of literature
2. the sound of the voice
3. variety
4. how high or low the voice sounds
5. It rises.
6. It increases.
7. everyone in the audience must hear every word
8. changing pitch within a sentence
9. a question
10. a regular reoccurring flow of sound and silence; pattern of stressed and unstressed syllables in a sentence
11. count of syllables in a line
12. poetry
13. overall sound of the voice

Oral Interpretation: Crossword Puzzle (page 76)

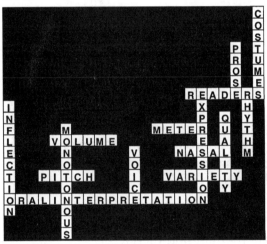

Pantomime (page 78)

1. communicating without words
2. face, hands, body posture
3. nothing
4. skill and training
5. pantos
6. they use words
7. It uses no words so it doesn't need to be translated. Everyone understands mime.
8. relax physically, gain better control of the body, move and gesture better, appear natural

9. commedia del' arte
10. (any two of the following) Charlie Chaplin, Buster Keaton, Laurel and Hardy

Improvisation (page 81)

1. to sharpen performance skills
2. think quickly, make interesting choices, encourage creativity, develop concentration, develop team work (any three)
3. guides the group, gives beginning situation, coaches, gives helpful suggestions, adds or changes information, decides when to end (any three)
4. to get used to working as a team
5. suggestions
6. memorize it
7. overpreparing and over planning
8. a conflict
9. (choose from the following) remember it is not a competition, requires teamwork, everyone must contribute, members must help each other, use imagination without fear of failure, provide things to build upon, avoid negative words and actions, do not become embarrassed or discouraged

Writing a Play (page 84)

1. playwright (not write)
2. play writing
3. 15 minutes to one hour
4. shows things happening
5. plot
6. character
7. theme
8. setting
9. time, perhaps season
10. dialogue
11. lines
12. action
13. conflict